How to Improve Your Financial Story: a Biblical Approach

2022
L.E. Peeples

ISBN 9798793395212

God is my refuge and strength,
a very present help in trouble.
Psalms 46:1

Table of Contents

Introduction

My name is Lori Porter-Peeples, the owner of Genesis Professional Services a bookkeeping and financial business service that started in 1985. This workbook was designed initially to compliment my church eGroup and guide participants on tithing, stewardship, creating and following a budget, investments and legacies, utilizing principles from the Word of God.

This financial plan is for those who would like to be able to get out of debt, pay some bills, save money for a rainy day, and have enough to be a blessing to their children, family, and friends. We do talk briefly about investments but do not make recommendations on retirement plans or other money investments, except to urge you to seek the advice of a Financial Advisor.

When you hear someone say, "we're going to talk about Financial Planning," what comes to your mind? For me, I think it's going to be a boring conversation about how I should set aside hundreds of dollars for the future, not considering what I need currently to run my household. Or if it is in regard to tithing, how I should give ten percent of my income no matter what, even if it means not paying the electric bill. I always wondered how much of a testimony it would be if you pay your tithes, but your lights were shut off for nonpayment. Here we'll learn to budget properly to be able to give as we are blessed to give, no matter the amount or percentage.

After reviewing other financial plans, I wanted to design one that was simple without being simplistic, but personal from the viewpoint of someone who struggled financially, stayed in a shelter, and filed bankruptcy, yet by the Grace of God and the guidance of the Holy Spirit was able to turn things around, improve my credit score, and be a blessing to my children and grandchildren. It's not a complicated story, it's a God story and I want to share it with you, that's what makes it different, not so much my story but how you can improve your finances and make it your story.

Jesus is the center of *How to Improve your Financial Story*. From the beginning it's important to know that everything is grounded in the Word of God. Why? Because what I accomplished was only through Christ.

So how, exactly, do we accept Jesus in our life? The answer is that we must believe in Him. This means placing confidence in the person of Christ, knowing that His death on Calvary's cross paid for all our sin. This is not merely an intellectual understanding; rather, it is a total surrender to Jesus as the only one who can forgive our sins, thereby bridging the gap between us and the Father. And when we receive Jesus as Savior, we immediately become children of the King. *Intouch.org Daily Devotional March 25, 2019, A Decision to Follow Jesus*

Romans 10 speaks of God's desire for His people to be saved. He acknowledges their enthusiasm but considers it as "misdirected zeal". Why? Because instead of understanding God's way of reconciliation to Himself, they try to connect to God by attempting to keep the Law or create their own personal way to be right with Him. Verse 4 tell us why our own personal way is futile:

> **For Christ has already accomplished the purpose for which the law was given. Romans 10:4**

Now, and only now, because of Christ we can be right with God, not by any actions of ourselves. Maybe deep down we already know that, because verse 8 says, "the Word of faith is near, even close at hand, and not only that, but it is in our mouth and in our hearts, that is why we can take the next step.

> **If you confess with your mouth, "Jesus is Lord," and believe in your heart that God raised him from the dead, you will be saved. Romans 10:9**

With your heart you believe that you are made right with God and by openly confessing your faith in Jesus Christ, you are saved. Doesn't that seem simple, but I Corinthians 1:18 says, "the message of the cross is foolishness to those who are perishing, but to us who are being saved it is the power of God."

What does it mean to be saved? Saved is an act of salvation, a verb, to be rescued. From what? To put it bluntly, saved from hell's fire. That should not be your only reason for wanting to be saved, but everyone goes somewhere when they die, and eternal life with Christ in heaven in the place He has prepared for me, sounds better than eternal burning and complete separation from God. What about you? The bottom line is to make a decision and make the wise choice, because…

> **"Everyone who calls on the name of the Lord will be saved." Romans 10:9**

Dear Heavenly Father, Thank you for giving us the privilege of choosing Christ. You are magnificent in all Your ways. Help us to hear the Holy Spirit's guidance as we set our minds on glorifying You in our Finances. Without You we can do nothing, with You we can do all things. In Jesus name we pray.

Topics

What is your financial story?

Tithing

Stewardship: Being a godly Steward

Reviewing your Credit Report

Managing Debt

Creating a Budget

Following your Budget

Investments

Legacy

Going Forward

> **For a great and effective door has opened to me, and *there* are many adversaries. I Corinthians 16:9**

When you decide to begin improving your financial story, don't think that a red carpet will roll out, the waters will part, and the storms will pass away, in celebration of your wise choice, probably just the opposite. As Paul stated, a door is opening for you, which means that God is providing you with the desire to improve your finances, and the knowledge and wisdom to do that in His Word. Dr. Charles Stanley said, "Wisdom is seeing things from God's perspective." And wisdom will help us improve our finances.

Paul also stated there are many adversaries, or should we say roadblocks or excuses. Isn't that always the case when you get ready to start a new project or make improvements in your life, you can think of a million excuses to start tomorrow, or better yet on Monday. Change is difficult and we know improving our finances won't be easy, but where does it say in the Word anything will be easy? It does say:

> **I can do all things through Christ who strengthens me. Philippians 4:13**

Yes, we can do all things, because our dependance is not on ourselves, but on Christ who gives us the strength to continue and persevere, never giving up. What are the possibilities with God? Think for a moment about the story of Elizabeth who was barren. Does that remind you of your finances, barren, empty, unproductive, fruitless? But when an angel told Mary about Elizabeth's approaching birth in her old age, verse 37 of Luke 1 says, "For with God nothing will be impossible." I'm sure Elizabeth in her old age did not think having a child was possible.

Or when Jesus was speaking of the rich young ruler about the Kingdom of Heaven and his disciples asked, "Who then can be saved?" Jesus replied in Luke 18:27:

> **The things which are impossible with men are possible with God.**

Or put another way, Matthew 19:26b says, "With men this is impossible, but with God all things are possible." I'm sure by now you get the point that with God things are possible, and that definitely includes our finances.

Maybe you have tried in the past and things did not work, should you try again? Yes of course. I wanted a healthy credit score, but I kept running into setback after setback, and no matter how hard I tried, I could never get ahead. My mother would say, "you take one step forward and two steps back", or you have to "rob Peter to pay Paul." Romans 5:3,4 really helped me because I realized that setbacks give meaning to struggles once we realize the purpose God has for those struggles.

> **But we also glory in tribulations, knowing that tribulation produces perseverance; and perseverance, character; and character, hope.**

Now I believe the Bible, but when it says I'm to glory in tribulations, I had to ask the Holy Spirit to help me understand the meaning. It took a while, but I finally saw that the tribulations, trials, setbacks, distress, pressures, and troubles were leading somewhere, in other words they had a purpose, to produce perseverance, character, and hope.

That's why you have to try again and keep trying, again and again if necessary. Because all you have been through is producing something in you. Webster describes perseverance as "to continue a course of action, in spite of difficulty or opposition." That sounds like not quitting to me. But that's not all, when we don't quit and we persevere we build character, moral strength. The Amplified Bible calls character "Spiritual Maturity". So, the struggles, if you don't quit, help you to grow spiritually. And God is so good, He adds the cherry on the top - Hope. When you have hope you can continue, because you are believing that the end is going to be better than the beginning. Hope reminds me of Hebrews 11:1.

> **Now faith is the substance of things hoped for, the evidence of things not seen.**

Faith and Hope are linked together, that's why we can never quit. I'm sure there is something in your life you are hoping for and maybe need improved finances to obtain what you are hoping for. That's where faith comes in, because we are hoping for something, but it's not seen at this present time. God is able to bring that hope through faith into reality, if you believe it's possible. And we just read all things with God are possible because in the end with God we are going to win. We are not talking about a "pie in the sky", there will be ups and downs, heartaches and pains, but through it all, all the tribulations, perseverance, character building, and hope, we can make it through and not only improve our finances but grow in the knowledge and understand of God our Father. Let's begin our journey.

Dear Heavenly Father, You give us Faith and Hope to keep pressing on despite difficulties. We are not depending on ourselves, but your strength to see us through and your guidance to show us the way. We love you Jesus. Amen.

What is your financial story?

While living in New York I had a small Bible group with the church I attended for about ten years. When I moved to Charlotte, I wanted to continue my group experience at my current church, however, the Lord spoke to my heart about sharing my experiences in a financial group, how He blessed me to go from bankruptcy in 2004 to purchasing two new-built homes in 2008 and in 2020, so others could be blessed as well. I looked over many plans including the Financial University, but I did not find one that spoke to me, and through the guidance of the Holy Spirit I pulled together this study on *How to Improve your Financial Story*. Yes, this workbook began around my story, but I believe Romans 2:11 "For God does not show favoritism." What He did for me is available to you as well.

As we go through each topic remember it's your story, think of each topic personally for you: how you feel about tithing, being a godly steward, where you stand with your credit history, elimination of debt, creating your budget, tips and strategies to follow your budget, it's all about you. And what you put in will determine what you get out, it's called ROI (Return on Investment) in yourself. That's about the only accounting term in this guide, because our focus is on practicality and how to get from point A to point B. Of course, there is tons of information on the internet if you want in depth Accounting Terminology or more Finance specifics, but my goal is to keep everything simple and understandable so that everyone can follow along.

When we talk about finances, we normally think rich, poor, middle class, upper class, sometimes barely making ends meet, or having just enough to get by. Oftentimes when it comes time to paying bills, we find ourselves, "robbing Peter to pay Paul". Did you ever wonder why? Or as the Bible puts it, knowing the truth about why you don't have enough. In John 8:32 – Jesus said, "you will know the truth, and the truth will set you free." Yes, knowing the truth will set you free, simply because you are aware of where you stand, not knowing the truth or facing the truth, can lead to more bondage. In other words, God reveals truth so we can apply truth to our lives and not continue to stumble in the dark. How? Through the power of the Holy Spirit who leads, guides, instructs, and encourages us, if we listen.

We will discuss more about truth in regard to finances when we get to the topic on reviewing your credit report, not to embarrass or worry you, but to begin to look at what is true and where you stand financially.

Think about how you currently feel about your finances, do you categorize yourself negatively or positively? Here is a question to think about:

How do you see yourself financially? Would you see your Financial Story as a Comedy, Drama, Horror, Action, or Romance? Christian? Why?

_____

_____

What financial goals do you hope to attain from this workbook?

_____

_____

_____

Being able to look at your Financial Story as a part of you that does not determine your overall worth or value is very important. I Corinthians 12:12-31 describes the parts of the body and how they function together as one member but many parts. Your finances are one aspect of you, so is being a parent, husband or wife, sister or brother, lawyer or doctor, student or homemaker, even kind and loving, and so on. We all have various titles, gifts, and characteristics given by God, with a goal to bring Him glory. Improving our finances is just another facet of how we can lift up the name of Jesus through our testimony and success.

Reflecting on your financial condition helps to reveal how you reached this stage while taking steps to change or improve your direction. My mother used to always say, "no need to cry over spilled milk." We can't turn back the hands of time and "un-spill" the milk, but we can move forward by cleaning up the milk and being more careful that we don't spill anymore milk.

Everyone can face troubling times financially, but don't despair, we as Christians have Jesus Christ as our Advocate, who said in John 16:33, "I have told you these things, so that in me you may have peace. In this world you will have trouble. But take heart! I have overcome the world." In other words, we don't have to be troubled, even though we have trouble, that's amazing and something you may need to ponder on deeply. But because of Christ overcoming, He provides a way for us to overcome as well.

It reminds me of the Bible story when the disciples were in the midst of a storm with waves and winds violently crashing against the boat (Mark 4), and Jesus was sleeping quietly in the "hinder" part of the boat. I can imagine seeing Jesus asleep on a pillow, but the disciples were panicking, similar to how I used to feel about my finances, and maybe you do now. They asked Jesus, "don't you care that we are about to perish?" Do you ever feel like that, maybe like you're drowning in debt and bills with no one or nothing helping you? Jesus solved their problem simply by saying, "Peace be still" and there was a great calm. Won't He do it for you too?

Now that's what I'm talking about, peace in the midst of a storm, you can have that when Jesus is onboard your lifeboat. Unfortunately, many times we find ourselves fretting and worrying about paying bills, and making ends meet, instead of realizing who is onboard. In verse :40 Jesus asked, "Why are you so fearful' How is it that you have no faith?" He equated being fearful with having no faith. If we ask our Father for help dealing with our finances, we must have faith to believe that He will help us, otherwise we'll end up tossed and driven with the storms of life wondering where is our help?

I will lift up my eyes to the hills – from whence comes my help? My help comes from the LORD, who made heaven and earth. Psalms 121:1,2

As Believers, we are blessed to have Jesus onboard in our lives and the Peace that He brings. Do you have Peace when it comes to your finances? Your financial story has more to do with your relationship with Christ working through your life, then it does how much money you have. Applying the Word of God changes Your story.

For the word of God is living and powerful, and sharper than any two-edged sword, piercing even to the division of soul and spirit, and of joints and marrow, and is a discerner of the thoughts and intents of the heart. Hebrews 4:12

Because the word of God is living and powerful, I can apply it to my life and you can apply it to your life, and it will be different how it works in my life and different how it works in your life. The word reaches deep down in our souls and helps us to discern what is really going on, not only with our finances, but with our life.

Dear Father, please guide us on our financial journey with your living word. Remove all fear and doubt as we trust Your magnificent power and grace. Help us listen to the Holy Spirit as He reveals all truth through Jesus Christ our Lord. Amen.

9

Foundational Scriptures

Reading the Word of God can help you focus more on the power available through the Holy Spirit than focusing on your circumstances. Here are some scriptures which are referred to throughout How to Improve your Finances. Take a few moments to read them and write some notes, maybe even bookmark this page for encouragement on your financial journey, then when you come upon difficult times and need a Word to see you through, you can refer to these scriptures, or add your own favorites.

Philippians 4:19	**And my God shall supply all your need according to His riches in glory by Christ Jesus.**
Matthew 6:33	But seek first the kingdom of God and His righteousness, and all these things shall be added to you.
John 10:10	The thief does not come except to steal, and to kill, and to destroy. I have come that they may have life, and that they may have *it* more abundantly.
Ephesians 3:20	**Now to Him who is able to do exceedingly abundantly above all that we ask or think, according to the power that works in us.**
Proverbs 3:5,6	**Trust in the Lord with all you heart and lean not on your own understanding; In all your ways acknowledge Him, and He shall direct your paths.**

How can the scriptures above encourage you about your finances? _____

_____

_____

Dear Father, thank you for love and grace, please guide us as we allow your Word to guide us into your Truth and give us peace as we wait on financial changes in our lives. You have always provided all our needs, help us to continue to trust you and seek your Kingdom first as we appreciate the abundant life you have provided. In Jesus name we pray.

Tithing

What comes to mind when you think of tithing? Is it positive or negative? Oftentimes when Tithing is mentioned, it produces feelings of dread or negativity. Maybe it's just my circle of friends and relatives, since tithing is not a conversation we can bring up without debate. And someone always says that they are "not giving money to a preacher for them to get rich." Maybe you have encountered other comments about tithing.

Yet as we endeavor to Improve our Finances, tithing has to be a part of the plan, mainly because our Father provides for us and is always giving, so should we do the same? The word "give" is mentioned in over 795 verses in the Bible. Therefore, it is understandable that giving is an important aspect of Christianity. Here are a few:

To give light on the earth – Genesis 1:15	Give us this day our daily bread – Matthew 6:11
Listen now to my voice, I will give you counsel – Exodus 18:19	He shall give His angels charge over you – Luke 4:10
To give you their land as an inheritance – Deuteronomy 4:38	My peace I give to you – John 14:27
Give thanks to the Lord for He is good – I Chronicles 16:34	So, let each one give as he purposes in his heart – II Corinthians 9:7
May the Lord give you wisdom and understanding? – I Ch 22:12	In everything give thanks, for this is the will of God in Christ Jesus for you - I Thessalonians 5:18
Give us help from trouble – Psalms 60:11	And behold, I am coming quickly, and My reward is with Me, to give to everyone according to his work – Rev 22:12
To give them beauty for ashes – Isaiah 61:3	
I will give you a new heart – Ezekiel 36:26	

One scripture in particular spoke to my heart, "And you shall remember the Lord your God, for it is He who gives you power to get wealth," **Deuteronomy 8:18a**. So, if God provides, and we know He freely gives, even the ultimate sacrifice of His Son Jesus, then what is our part? Should we just receive always and not give?

Through the Lord's mercies we are not consumed, because His compassions fail not. They are new every morning; Great is Your faithfulness. Lamentations 3:22-23

Tithing provides a way for us to participate in God's mighty plan. Our focus should not be should I give 5%, 10%, or 50%, whether it's before or after taxes, only to give freely. In **Mark 10,** Jesus counsels the rich young ruler who asked what did he have to do to inherit eternal life? Jesus spoke about keeping the commandments. I'm sure the young man felt very confident, because he stated he had "kept" them all since his youth.

That's amazing in itself that he could keep all the commandments. But it had to be something else, because we know that we cannot keep the law or commandments on our own. Jesus wasn't mad at him because he was disingenuous, verse 21 said Jesus "looked at him with love." How great is the compassion of Christ? Jesus did mention there was one thing he lacked. You would think that if the young man kept all the commandments, he was well on his way to winning the approval of Christ. However, Jesus told him, "One thing you lack" Go your way, sell whatever you have and give to the poor, and you will have treasure in heaven; and come, take up the cross, and follow Me."

Should we give all we have to the poor? Jesus was making a point about what truly was important to the rich young ruler, it wasn't so much about keeping the commandments, even though he thought he did, it was more about where his heart and focus was, in his case, the riches he had accumulated. Jesus advised him to get rid of what was really his treasure and follow Him. Giving away everything must have been very difficult, because verse 22 says, "but he was sad at this word, and went away sorrowful, for he had great possessions." Our direction should not be to give all we have to the poor, but we do have to have our priorities straight and giving/tithing, is an important part of a Christian financial plan. How do you know how much to give? Each person has to consult with the Holy Spirit to determine what they should give. Has God spoken to you about Tithing and how much to give?

Write some notes on your thoughts about tithing: _____

_____

_____

_____

_____

Generally speaking, a tithe is 10% of income, some debate whether you calculate the amount before or after taxes, ask the Holy Spirit for guidance for you. Some are able to tithe 10%, some are able to be even more generous and tithe more. One quote from Pastor Andy Stanley in a message on tithing, "But if you ask God, He will show you how to honor Him with everything you have. Not just with a percentage of it, but with all of it." Faithfulness, generosity, and consistency are key to whatever your decision is for the amount to give.

In *How to Improve your Financial Story*, the goal was to present some Old Testament and New Testament scriptures regarding tithing, and for you, the reader, through prayer, to determine your direction. My thoughts are that tithing is personal between a person and God, and nowhere did I read in the Bible that tithing or not tithing should be a source of guilt. Guilt comes if you compare what you give to what others give. Your gift is personal between you and God.

Those who have been in church awhile are familiar with Malachi 3:10

> **Bring all the tithes into the storehouse, that there may be food in My house, and try Me now in this", says the LORD of hosts, "If I will not open for you the windows of heaven and pour out for you such blessing that there will not be room enough to receive it."**

Here is another helpful scripture that talks about providing your "first fruits" which simply means to give to God first before other obligations. That takes discipline, budgeting, and planning which we will get to when we discuss creating a budget.

> **Honor the Lord with your possessions, and with the first fruits of all your increase; so, your barns will be filled with plenty, and your vats will overflow with new wine. Proverbs 3:9,10**

What I try to do when giving my first fruits is to have my tithes and offerings automatically taken out each month. That way other budget items do not interfere with how much I have set aside to give. One question often asked is did Jesus say you should tithe. In this passage, He clearly answers if we should tithe, as well as what is even more important when it comes to giving.

> **But how terrible it will be for you Pharisees! For you are careful to tithe even the tiniest part of your income, but you completely forget about justice and the love of God. You should tithe, yes, but you should not leave undone the more important things. Luke 11:42**

In my research, there was a lot of debate about tithing being an Old Testament thing and was not in the New Testament. Jesus said specifically in verse 42: You should tithe, yes", maybe that ends the debate. However, He did add a "but". It seems tithing is a package deal, meaning it's not only about giving a percentage of earnings, but it also includes other attributes like justice and the love of God. In Matthew 23:23, He adds mercy and faith. So, yes Jesus said we should tithe, but we should also show love, mercy, justice, and faith.

This brings up a great question, what does God want from us in relation to offerings and sacrificial giving? Here is one answer I found in I Samuel 15:22 in a conversation between Samuel and Saul:

> **But Samuel replied, what is more pleasing to the LORD: your burnt offerings and sacrifices or your obedience to His voice? Listen! Obedience is better than sacrifice, and submission is better than offering the fat of rams.**

Obviously, we don't offer up ram fat to God, but I'm sure unless you are very rich, everything we offer to the Lord is a sacrifice. But it is interesting to note that obedience was more important than sacrifice and that submission to God is better than an offering. Has God mentioned any areas that you need to submit to Him? Are there areas in your life where you lack obedience?

There are various ways God speaks to us, through the Holy Spirit, scriptures, our Pastors, Creation, difficulties, or whomever or whatever He chooses. One thing for sure, when God speaks it is always in alignment with His Word and His Will for our lives. Listen. Are you able to determine what God is saying for your life when it comes to tithing? It is more likely to be a soft whisper instead of a loud shout over television, music, conversations, or other things going on in your life. Often, you have to find some quiet time or a quiet place to hear what God is speaking.

Hosea 6:6 offers more insight to what God is requiring, similar to what Jesus said:

> **For I desire mercy and not sacrifice, and the knowledge of God more than burnt offerings.**

Sometimes we get caught up in our giving or tithing, yet when we examine our lives, we can see personally that there are other characteristics to focus on. How would you describe mercy in your life? Are you showing mercy to others? What if you feel they don't deserve mercy? Aren't you thankful we have the mercy of God? I always remember Grace and Mercy together. Grace is God giving us what we don't deserve, and Mercy is God not giving us what we do deserve. Are there times when you should have shown Mercy? And how do we obtain the "knowledge of God"?

Reflect for a moment on ways to show mercy and know God better:

_____

_____

_____

When it comes to giving, this scripture represents the bottom line on how to give:

Each of you should give what you have decided in your heart to give, not reluctantly or in response to pressure, for God loves a cheerful giver. II Corinthians 9:7

Several points can be gathered from this scripture:
1) Give as he/she purposes in their heart – To be able to give without guilt or feeling intimidated, what you give has to be your decision between you and the Holy Spirit.
2) Not grudgingly or of necessity (KJV) – giving grudgingly means you really don't feel comfortable giving a certain amount and maybe you really don't want to give at all but feel it's a necessity or you have to give or feel pressured to give maybe because others are giving.
3) What does God love? – that should be our motivation, how can our giving please God? When we give cheerfully. Of course, you want your funds to be used appropriately for the Kingdom of God, and maybe that requires some investigation into knowing where your organization gives after they receive, but no matter who you give to, do it cheerfully as if giving to the Lord.

Finally, before you give, Jesus explained the appropriate attitude in Matthew 5:23:

So, if you are presenting a sacrifice at the altar in the Temple and you suddenly remember that someone has something against you, leave your sacrifice there at the altar. Go and be reconciled to that person. Then come and offer your sacrifice to God.

In the Bible, giving is not only about dropping a few dollars in the offering plate. Jesus emphasized that we should examine ourselves before giving our offering. We know when we have something against someone, or even when they have something against us. How do we know? Because the Holy Spirit will bring it to your

17

remembrance. If you hurt someone, how long does it take for you to apologize? Do you apologize right away or just try to forget about it? Sometimes when we are hurt and waiting on the other person to apologize, they might not. Then what do you do? In that case, you can't control what someone does, even when you want them to apologize. Many times, I have had to go and be reconciled to someone, and I was not at fault, in my eyes anyway. But no matter who was at fault, apologizing when either party is offended will keep you in right relationship with them and the Lord. Anger and grudges are best left behind. Don't let the sun go down on your anger. Especially since Jesus says in Matthew 5:22, "But I tell you that anyone who is angry with a brother or sister will be subject to judgement."

That brings a totally different perspective to giving. Ask yourself are you holding anything against someone? It's best to apologize and move on, so we can give our offering freely and cheerfully, because God forgives our debts as we forgive our debtors. And remember, Jesus paid it all, why then should we harbor unforgiveness.

My prayer is that these scriptures shed more light on tithing and that your decision is not only based on an amount or percentage of the money you earn, but based on giving with a clean heart, the right attitude, a godly character, and cheerfully.

Have your views on Tithing changed? _____

_____

_____

Have you decided how much you will budget for Tithing? Why? _____

_____

_____

_____

Dear Father, help us to participate in tithing and giving cheerfully as a way to show our love and obedience to You. May our giving reflect the generosity we have received from your grace and mercy. In all things we will give thanks because You are a good Father. In Jesus name we pray.

Stewardship

What comes to mind when you think of being a godly Steward?

_____

_____

_____

Preparing for *How to Improve your Financial Story,* I found this on being godly. I am not trying to plagiarize someone's words, so if you recognize this let me know and I will add the author, because I honestly don't remember where I saw it, and of course I should have written the bibliographical notes immediately, but I didn't, still it is worth sharing:

How to be godly, does it depend on how you feel?

This will really shock you: Sometimes I don't feel like praying or reading my Bible. But I do it. I've found that if the only time I <u>pray</u> is when I feel like it, the devil makes sure I never feel like it. If the only time I <u>read</u> my Bible is when I feel like it, the devil makes sure I never feel like it. Maturity is when you live your life by your commitments, not by your feelings.

In the same way, you don't become a godly man or woman by simply doing what you feel like doing. Godly men and women choose to develop the habits that produce godliness in their lives.

I'm always grabbing my Webster's dictionary, which I love, probably because some definitions are so simple. The definition for godly is "devoted to God". Simple as that. Therefore, I would consider myself a godly person, in no way shape or form am I saying that I am perfect, or have arrived in the realm of Christianity, but I am devoted to God. Paul says it better in Philippians 3:12-14, that we are not perfect, but we keep pressing on, not looking back and never giving up.

I don't mean to say that I have already achieved these things or that I have already reached perfection. But I press on to possess that perfection for which Christ Jesus first possessed me. No, dear brothers and sisters, I have not achieved it, but I focus on this one thing: Forgetting the past and looking forward to what lies ahead, I press on to reach the end of the race and receive the heavenly prize for which God, through Christ Jesus, is calling us.

And I believe if you are reading this book and diligently seeking Christ to improve your finances through study and following the guidance of the Holy Spirit, you are godly as well. Amen.

We all want to be useful in the Kingdom of God and of course there is a place for everyone to serve. But how can you know if you are being a godly Steward and utilizing the gifts and talents God has given you in the way He wants you to use them as a servant to the Kingdom. In Mark 10:45, Jesus speaks of His ultimate service, "For even the Son of Man did not come to be served, but to serve, and to give His life as a ransom for many." As we follow our Leader, Jesus Christ, how can we serve? I'm sure God has already brought something to your mind. Maybe you are wondering where to get started or what does it mean to be a godly steward.

One explanation I found was from Pastor Charles Stanley,

"Stewardship is faithful management of the time, talents, spiritual gifts, and treasures God has given us. They are to be used according to His priorities and direction, not for our own self-advancement." *Intouch.org Daily Devotional January 13, 2022, Discovering Life's Purpose*

Spend some time reflecting on the areas in your life God has given you to steward over or serve. Write some notes for each and what you can do to improve. Also include any scriptures God lays on your heart as you meditate about the following:

Time – How do you spend your time spiritually? What can you do to improve?

_____

_____

_____

Talents – What are your God-given Talents? How are you using them?

_____

_____

_____

_____

Spiritual Gifts – What are your spiritual gifts? How are you using them?

_____

_____

_____

Treasures – How are you using the treasures God provides?

_____

_____

_____

Why do we Serve?

> **For we are His workmanship, created in Christ Jesus for good works, which God prepared beforehand that we should walk in them.   Ephesians 2:10**

This is so clear that we are created in Christ Jesus for good works, and not only that, but God prepared what we would do beforehand. So why do we serve, because we were created to serve and do good works. Are you serving? If not, then why?

Love should be our primary motivation, not out of obligation or to be seen by others as "workers in the church", but because we genuinely care for the people we are serving. I Corinthians 13: 1-3 lets us know what happens if we don't have love.

> **Though I speak with the tongues of men and of angels, but have not love, I have become sounding brass or a clanging cymbal. And though I have _the gift_ of prophecy, and understand all mysteries and all knowledge, and though I have all faith, so that I could move mountains, but have not love, I am nothing. And though I bestow all my goods to feed the _poor,_ and though I give my body to be burned, but have not love, it profits me nothing.**

Are you attempting to move mountains in the church by doing everybody's job, or giving away all your money to the poor? Unfortunately, the Bible say it means nothing if you don't have love. That sounds like futile service with no potential for gain, or a better picture is a dog or cat chasing their tail, around and around in a circle, getting nowhere. We all say, "love you" all the time, when we end a phone call or say good-bye. Love is used very freely in our society and sometimes you wonder when a person speaks of love are they genuine. Here is a test to find out if it is really Love from I Corinthians 13:4-7.

> Love is patient, love is kind. It does not envy, it does not boast, it is not proud. It does not dishonor others, it is not self-seeking, it is not easily angered, it keeps no record of wrongs. Love does not delight in evil but rejoices with the truth. It always protects, always trusts, always hopes, always perseveres.

Three main sources of Love:

GOD – God is love, and he who abides in love abides in God, and God in him.

I John 4:16b

The Holy Spirit – But the fruit of the Spirit is love. Galatians 5:22a

Jesus – (Jesus is speaking) "A new commandment I give to you, that you love one another; as I have loved you, that you also love one another." John 13:34

The more we get to know the Trinity and the love they have for us, the more we will desire to share our experiences with others through service. While serving, we glorify God and become a testimony to others and a light to those in darkness.

How do we Serve?

First service begins with an attitude to serve, glad to be able to participate in the advancement of the Kingdom of God. To do this we need the love of God, and we also need the wisdom of God. Godly wisdom or discernment doesn't just happen and one day we wake up wise, it has to be sought after by spending time in scriptures. David had an awesome relationship with the Father as evident in the Psalms:

> When You said, "Seek My face," my heart said to You, "Your face, Lord, I will seek. Psalms 27:8

In this passage, God told David, "Seek My face," and David's heart responded that he would seek God's face. You begin to gain wisdom by seeking after God and the Word fills your heart and mind, then the Lord begins to reveal Himself and your discernment grows as you grow in Christ allowing you to serve effectively.

Seeking God sounds simple enough, but how do you go about finding God? I found a great explanation in the *Intouch.org Daily Devotional April 29, 2022, How to seek God:* "Start with the Scriptures and prayer. Set aside time each day for meditating on God's Word: Listen for His voice, slowly digest what you read, talk to the Lord, ask Him Questions, and apply what you learn." Here is an analogy of Wisdom.

Don't turn your back on wisdom, for she will protect you. Love her, and she will guard you. Getting wisdom is the wisest thing you can do! Proverbs 4:6-7

When we seek God, we'll grow in wisdom. The next step is very important, sharing the wisdom we have received with others. Remember we have the Good News; Jesus Christ is the answer for the world today. When someone looks at you in service, does your face reflect the joy and peace of Christ, making them cry out, "what must I do to be saved?" Our walk and how others see us can be very challenging, but we can do this by renewing our minds in the Word of God and demonstrating God's will by loving those we serve. Romans 12:2 puts it this way:

And do not be conformed to this world, but be transformed by the renewing of your mind, that you may prove what *is* that good and acceptable and perfect will of God.

And we can serve gladly because we have presented our bodies as a living sacrifice, holy and acceptable to God (verse 1). This is our "reasonable service". NLT says, "This is truly the way to worship Him." What better way to worship than service.

One great example of stewardship is the parable of the talents of gold given by Jesus in Matthew 25:14-18.

For the *Kingdom of heaven* is like a man traveling to a far country, who called his own servants and delivered his goods to them. And to one he gave five talents, to another two, and to another one, to each according to his own ability; and immediately he went on a journey. Then he who had received the five talents went and traded with them and made another five talents. And likewise, he who had received two gained two more also. But he who had received one went and dug in the ground and hid his lord's money.

Here we have three servants who were given different "talents" of monetary value and were responsible to the master for what they would do with what they were given. Jesus starts off by saying this parable describes the "Kingdom of Heaven". In other words, Jesus is the Master, who travelled away to a "far country" and while He was away, He gave the servants the necessary resources to accomplish the mission until the time when He returns, when the accounts would be "settled with them (verse 19)."

You know the story, when he returned the one with five gained five more talents, the one with two gained two more. In other words, they increased what that had, and the Master received a return on His investment. And both received the reply, "Well done, good and faithful servant; you were faithful over a few things, I will make you ruler over many things. Enter into the joy of your Lord." That is definitely what we want to hear, not so much for the other servant who did not do anything with his talent but only hid it away and didn't use his talent and was referred to as a "wicked and lazy servant".

We all have at least one talent. Finding our talent and using it to the glory of God is our goal. One thing I hope to take away from *How to Improve Your Financial Story* is the importance of having a *relationship* with God our Father because when we cultivate a relationship, no one has to tell us to read our Bible, or volunteer, give donations, serve, or even to love one another, because all of those things and more comes with knowing God, having Christ in our life, and listening to the Holy Spirit. God does not just send us out into the world unprepared, He gives us talents and gifts to complete our mission and be a light for Christ.

It's interesting to note that in verse 15 He gave the talents based on their "own ability", meaning He knew one would do well with five, the other with two, and the last with one. How do you fit into this story? Are you blessed with many talents you are using for the glory of God? Or do you have a few talents but faithful in service? Or are you still trying to figure out what your talents are, and in the process, you are not serving at all? Take a few moments to reflect:

_____

_____

_____

The Bible specifically names the gifts of the Holy Spirit. Take some time to identify your gifts, seeking the guidance of the Holy Spirit to find out how and where God wants to use the gifts He has provided. Don't leave your gift unopened.

Gifts of the Holy Spirit

When you think of service and finding your gifts, there are many Spiritual Assessment's online. Check to see if your church offers one, or you could use common sense. For instance, if you enjoy working with children, maybe volunteering in the children's ministry is for you. However, if you already have children and you would prefer to help as a Greeter, then that might be an option. If in service you find yourself struggling, stressed, or frustrated, ask yourself, are you utilizing your talent according to your ability that God has provided, or working in your own strength? Pastor Steven once said, "are you trying to fly as a bird when you are better suited to swim as a fish." Usually when we are working in God's talents it brings a rewarding feeling of accomplishment and peace, plus we are glad when it is our time to serve. Yes, somedays can be more difficult than others, but we can always find encouragement in what David said in Psalms 122:1:

I was glad when they said to me, "Let us go into the house of the Lord."

Your gift is based on your own ability as Jesus said in Matthew 25:15. Think about your characteristics and personal attributes as you look over the list below. Remember, God knows which gift is best suited for the purpose He has for your life. It is good to know how many you have, but it is more important to use your gifts in service according to God's will, link up with the Holy Spirit to know for sure.

Romans 12:6-8 tells us "we have different gifts, according to the grace given to each of us, and gives suggestions as to how to use that particular gift:

Prophesy – Speak out with as much faith as God has given you
Serving Others – Serve them well
Teacher – Teach them well
Encouraging Others – Be encouraging
Giving – Give generously
Leadership Ability – Take the responsibility seriously
Showing Kindness to Others – Do it gladly

Take some time to reflect over these gifts and how they apply to you: _____

_____

_____

> **God has given each of you a gift from his great variety of spiritual gifts. Use them well to serve on another. Do you have the gift of speaking? Then speak as though God himself were speaking through you. Do you have the gift of helping others? Do it with all the strength and energy that God supplies. Then everything you do will bring glory to God through Jesus Christ. I Peter 4:10-11**

One thing to remember, it is a privilege to serve God, the benefits are great, the pay is excellent, and the rewards are never-ending. Most importantly, we are participating in God's will for our lives by spreading and sharing the Gospel of Jesus Christ, all the while showing love to the world around us.

> **So, my dear brothers and sisters, be strong and immovable. Always work enthusiastically for the Lord, for you know that nothing you do for the Lord is ever useless. I Corinthians 15:58**

How do we link our financial story with our spiritual story and being a godly steward? I found a quote from Tony Evans in "Getting a Steward's Perspective", and he said, "If your financial life is going up but your spiritual life is going down, then you have become ensnared by the love and pursuit of money." And we definitely don't want that.

Does it really matter how much money you have? Or is being able to pay your bills, have money for family and relaxation and live a peaceful godly life enough? When it comes to wealth and contentment, the NLT makes the same scripture very plain:

> **Yet true godliness with contentment is itself great wealth. After all, we brought nothing with us when we came into the world, and we can't take anything with us when we leave it. So, if we have enough food and clothing, let us be content. I Timothy 6:6-8**

What is the goal of Your Financial Story? Is it centered around God and the plans He has for your life so that you may be a blessing to others? Or is it to benefit yourself and immediate family? There is nothing incorrect with either answer, take a few moments to reflect over these questions from your financial perspective.

_____

_____

Teach those who are rich in this world not to be proud and not to trust in their money, which is so unreliable. Their trust should be in God, who richly gives us all we need for our enjoyment. Tell them to use their money to do good. They should be rich in good works and generous to those in need, always being ready to share with others. By doing this they will be storing up their treasure as a good foundation for the future so they may experience true life. I Timothy 6:17-19

This scripture is an awesome summary for Stewardship and being a godly steward, it helps us keep our focus on God and not on our own wealth and riches. Are you content with what you have? Our Father knows what we need:

And my God shall supply all your need according to His riches in glory by Christ Jesus. Philippians 4:19

God richly gives us all we need, that is great right there, but He also says for our enjoyment. That's amazing, God wants us to enjoy what He has given us. Maybe that's how we can continue to do good works and help those in need, because we are content with what we have, and experience true life.

How are you using or not using your talents in being a godly steward?

_____

_____

_____

What are some ways you can improve?

_____

_____

Dear Father, please lead us by your Holy Spirit to know what to give and to give cheerfully. Help us to use the talents provided by your grace to glorify your name as we serve others, to ultimately hear your blessings of "well done my good and faithful servant". In Jesus name we pray.

Reviewing your Credit Report

What emotion is invoked when you think of your credit report? Is it fear or self-doubt because of past failures, or has it been so long since you looked at your report that you really don't know what you'll find? Now is the time to think about what Jesus said regarding truth in John 8:32, "And you shall know the truth, and the truth shall make you free." Webster's Dictionary gives a very blunt definition of truth, "conformity with fact, reality, actual existence, and that which is true."

You can't hide from the truth. Therefore, if you desire to *Improve your Financial Story,* you have to know the truth about where you stand financially, and that is where the credit report comes in. One side note, a credit report does not determine who you are, we are first and foremost children of God Most High, **El Elyon**. However, in the world we live in, it helps to know what is on your credit report, especially when various institutions utilize the information to determine if they will approve your request for loans, purchases, or other forms of credit worthiness.

When I moved to Charlotte, initially I intended to stay in a hotel while my home was being built, but quickly realized that was not going to work for me, so I began looking for an apartment. Yes, I did find one and it was expensive, but the point I want to make is, the apartment agency checked my credit. Then when I attempted to turn on the electricity, they checked my credit. The same for the cable, the water company, and the insurance company for renter's insurance. All I could do was thank God my credit had improved, because five years prior my low credit score would have prevented me from renting an apartment and turning on the utilities. I'm not ashamed to admit that in the 1990's my credit score was so poor that I had to turn the electricity on in my son's name. Have you ever had to do that? That was one way the truth began to set me free, because I was so embarrassed, I had to turn things around. I had to face what was causing the bondage on the way to freedom.

The current truth about your finances is found on your credit report, knowing what it says can help you understand where you are starting from financially. If your credit report is negative, then at least you know what is on your report that is causing it to be negative, because all the items are listed in detail, negative and positive. If there are items on your credit report that do not belong to you, then you have to take steps to have them removed, which we'll discuss how to do that later. If your credit report is positive, then Praise God. Remember, having credit is not a good or bad thing, but using credit to work for you is the goal.

Once you know the truth, what is the next step to being free. Jesus explained that in verse 31 when He said, "If you abide in My word, you are My disciples indeed." We are not only God's children, but followers of Christ, and continually spending time in the word, abiding, we'll be able to recognize truth and be free. As a disciple we are learners of Christ who focus our attention on seeking after the truth in order to experience for ourselves the freedom therein.

He goes on to talk about sin and being a slave to sin. When determining financial growth, debt is comparable to being a slave to sin. With excessive debt, we are slaves to whomever we own the debt too. Yes, being a slave to debt is extreme, but you can have debt that is managed properly as we'll discuss under budgeting. We all want debt to just be gone, but for some of us, we have to chip away at that debt, little by little, and that's okay. There is no magic wand to wave debt away, it's like the tortoise and the hare, slow and steady wins the race.

Did you find truth in reviewing your credit report? _____

_____

_____

So how do you begin to be free now that you know the truth? All holes have a way out. In fact, God said it better in I Corinthians 10:13:

> **The temptations in your life are no different from what others experience. And God is faithful, He will not allow the temptation to be more than you can stand. When you are tempted, he will show you a way out so that you can endure.**

That's good to know, that no matter what temptation you face, including financial, God gives you an escape route, so the temptation won't be overpowering. The question is will you take the way out?

What steps can you take to avoid the temptations of excessive debt _____

_____

_____

_____

Obtaining your Credit Report

If you haven't already, obtain your free credit report. And did I say "free", so if someone wants you to pay for your report, don't, it's a free report.

1) Go to annualcreditreport.com
2) Fill out a form with Name, Address, Birthdate, Social
3) If lived at Address less than 2 years, add second address
4) Select number of reports – Equifax, Experian, TransUnion (select all 3)
5) Once Report is ready your last 4 digits of Social is needed
6) You will have to answer some questions that only you should know to verify your identity. It took me 2 attempts. You have to get the answers correct to receive the report.
7) Once completed, the report will have your name (and all your names used for credit), your addresses, birthdate, phone numbers, employers, and all the accounts opened.
8) Click Print your Report (top right) or save as a PDF file for later review.
9) Save to your Computer or to a USB drive.

You have to pay to get your FICO Score, but now many credit card companies will provide your FICO score monthly.

Before we begin, please look over all the **names** listed, there can be many variations, first name last name, middle initial added, special spellings, but they all should be "your" names. If you see any names that do not belong to you, contact the credit reporting agency with your report number as a reference, listed on website as "Contact Us". Do the same review for **addresses**, making sure you are familiar with all the addresses listed, mine went back 30 years. Also make sure your "**year of birth**" is correct, and make sure there are no incorrect **phone numbers,** or strange numbers you don't recognize. The process to contact them is cumbersome, so don't waste time just to update phone numbers. **Employers** listed should be ones you have actually worked for, since potential creditors use this information to verify your employment.

At a Glance - shows the number of Accounts, Public Records, and Hard Inquiries Accounts – carefully review each account.

- Account Name – example American Express, or VISA
- Account Type – Credit or Charge Card, Mortgage, Auto Loan/Lease, Education loans

- Date Opened – make sure this is accurate or a reasonable estimate
- Status – this shows your payment history
- Status Updated – this is the last time the agencies updated your report
- Balance – this shows how much you owed at the last update
- Payments – amounts paid
- Credit Limit – how much you have available to use
- Highest Balance – monthly amount used on card

Accounts - More detail is included showing each month and the amount paid, as well as **Contact Info** for that particular account. This is good to review if you notice missing payments and you have receipts that you did make payments. That's why it is important to pay by check, or online where a payment history is kept. And if you do pay online, save your payment record on your computer. I usually keep a folder by year with all my bill payment receipts. You could pay with a money order, but you should save the receipt copy for your records in case there is a dispute? **Never pay with cash.**

If you have items on your Credit Report that need further review, investigation, or resolution, write below:

Account	Description	Amount	Resolved?

We said earlier that the Truth sets us free, here is an additional scripture to ponder in light of your freedom as it relates to debt.

> **Stand fast therefore in the liberty by which Christ has made us free, and do not be entangled again with a yoke of bondage. Galatians 5:1**

Get rid of debt. Get rid of debt. Get rid of debt. I hear that all the time, for some that is easier said than done, especially if you are working with a limited income, or raising a family as a single parent, or any of the other thousands of circumstances that hinder a person from simply getting rid of debt. We will discuss some ways to chip away at debt, but this one thing I do know, once you do get rid of debt or even begin reducing your debt, "do not be entangled again with a yoke of bondage."

I confess, over the years I did this several times with my JC Penney card. I would struggle and struggle to pay it off, all the while paying exorbitant amounts of interest, only finding myself charging hundreds of dollars during Christmas that I knew I couldn't pay off until June or July. I ended up entangled in bondage again. I'm not saying cut up your JC Penney card up, or any other card for that matter, but I am saying, if you do use your card, only spend what you can pay off before the bill is due, thereby not receiving any more interest charges on your account.

My daughter obtained her first credit card (after she got a job), and she asked me when should she pay her bill? I told her every time she gets paid, biweekly in her case, she should pay her bill off in full, that way she'll never incur a late charge, not will she incur finance charges. For me, I pay mine off monthly. One note, if you ever by chance receive a late fee on a credit card or other bill, call the company and ask for a courtesy removal, normally they give you at least one per year.

Another tip, always check your monthly credit or bank statement for hidden fees or added maintenance charges. Lately I received an $8 fee on my bank statement that I did not know was there until I did my month-end reconciliation. I couldn't figure out what it was for. My daughter said if they charge all their customers and only 20% complain, they'll earn a profit. Exactly! I immediately called and asked for that to be removed, or I'd have to close the account. Be prepared you'll get a recording who usually has difficulty understanding, and you definitely might be on the phone for quite some time. During this time, I have the call on speaker, and I'm occupied doing other things while waiting, but I'm not going to hang up until my situation is resolved.

Eventually someone answered and they explained that since my balance fell below $500, they had to charge me the $8 fee. I politely asked them to remove it, but they would not, so I closed the account. It was really not a problem since they only paid .02¢ monthly interest, and I had a different savings account that paid $3.00 monthly. Bottomline, check around for which institution will give you the most for holding your money and don't pay fees if they can be avoided. Most banks, if you have direct deposit, will give you a free no-fee checking account. Always shop around for the best deal because your money matters.

What is a FICO® Credit Score?

"FICO is the acronym for **Fair Isaac Corporation**, as well as the name for the credit scoring model that Fair Isaac Corporation developed." - *Cornell University*

Based on your credit history and other factors the FICO tool is used to create a credit score for you that lenders use to assess if you qualify for credit cards, mortgages, and other loans. Nowadays more and more agencies use FICO for things like car insurance, rental applications, even utilities. The three credit reporting agencies TransUnion, Equifax, and Experian, designate a credit score based on your financial history as follows:

Credit Score	Rating
800 – 850	Exceptional
740 – 799	Very Good
670 – 739	Good
580 – 669	Fair
300 – 579	Poor

Don't despair if you fall into a lower category. Remember a credit score is not who we are, it shows our situation financially, but because we are children of God, we can stand on the Word that says:

Now to Him who is able to do exceedingly abundantly above all that we ask or think, according to the power that works in us. Ephesians 3:20

God is able, no matter what the situation is, to turn things around. I'm not just saying that because it sounds good but from experience, because He did it for me and I know He can do it for you as well. After age 19 when I blew through all the credit cards that kept coming in the mail without paying the charges, my credit score dropped to the lowest point possible. Then when my middle daughter needed help financially in college, I wasn't able to provide her the assistance she needed, and it broke my heart. And when I did search around and finally obtained a loan for her, the interest rate was very high because of my poor credit score. But God did not keep me in that situation, through prayer and perseverance, which we will discuss in an upcoming topic, I was able to move my score from "Poor" to "Exceptional" and give my youngest daughter the assistance in college she needed. Not with a student loan but with tuition payments paid in full. How? Each month I would set aside an amount for her tuition so when the semester bill came, I was ready. It helped that she did not go to a very expensive school which made her tuition affordable. Then I was able to pay her semester with a credit card, paying it off before the bill was due with savings, thereby avoiding interest charges, in addition I earned 1% cash back. You might say 1% is not a lot. But 1% of $10,000 is $100.

Every credit score is unique for each individual, but the basic formula is the same for everyone:

Credit Score
Payment History: 35%
Amount Owed: 30%
Length of Credit History: 15%
New Credit Opened: 10%
Types of Credit: 10%

As you can see, payment history is the most important, it shows exactly when you pay month by month, so it's important not to miss a payment, nor have any late payments.

Here is a sample Credit score history, which you can find now on most credit card websites:

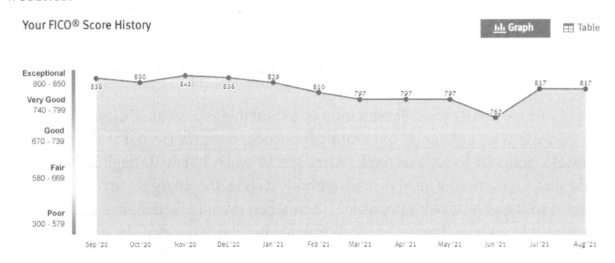

This is a one-year snapshot of how credit fluctuates monthly, yours maybe similar. Anytime you use your credit it could change your score. Mine changed when I paid my daughter's tuition, various credit inquiries when purchasing my home, purchases for furniture, but once I got back on my normal budget, my score began to return back to the exceptional range.

How did I go from bankruptcy in 2004 to exceptional credit in 2021? Step-by-Step, being consistent, never giving up paying your bills on time, avoiding late charges, and not frivolously using credit. There is no magic formula and many ups and downs, successes and failures, but it all starts with what you are doing now, trusting God and believing that He will guide you from step-to-step.

We will start in the next topic with managing current debt, then creating and following a budget, which is the most important step. As you can see from my timeline of 17 years, that it was a slow and steady process. Actually, it was not that long, because from 2004 until I purchased my home in 2008, I was just stumbling along, not really caring about credit. I felt all was lost because I had filed bankruptcy. It was only by God's grace that I was able to buy the home and maintain it. Rightfully so I should not have been able to because of poor credit and no deposit, but one day I just walked out on faith, and each step of the way, the lender said yes, I was shocked, but it wasn't me, it was the power of Christ working within me. The same can happen for you, walk out on faith, before you say no, you never know what God will do for you, but if you just figure you'll never reach your financial goals or buy a house, or pay off that debt, you're already defeated before you even find out what God would have done.

Which reminds of when the disciples saw Jesus walking on the water towards them, of course Peter wanted to walk on the water too. Of course, Jesus said, "Come".

> **But when Peter saw that the wind was boisterous, he was afraid; and beginning to sink he cried out, saying, "Lord, save me!" And immediately Jesus stretched out *His* hand and caught him, and said to him, "O you of little faith, why did you doubt?" Matthew 14:30-31**

Peter started off good, but then he started to look around, at the economy, the news report, the inflation rate, the interest rate, the blowing wind, and he started to sink. In other words, Peter took his eyes off Jesus to look around at circumstances. Do you do that? What we are striving for in *How to Improve your Financial Story* is to laser focus in on Christ, especially when the circumstances appear difficult.

Credit can be a trap and I fell into that trap several times throughout my life, and many of you most likely have similar stories. Mine began in college when everybody sent me a credit card. Unfortunately, my mom was no longer with me, so I had no idea about the trap, I was just a 19-year-old making purchases without even thinking of repayment. Until the bills began to pile up and I could not pay them. My next credit trap was when my children were growing up and I didn't have enough saved to purchase toys and clothes, so I bought everything on credit. I remember it clearly; I would buy presents for Christmas that took me until April to pay-off or later. All the while, the interest was accumulating at 26% or more, month after month, it was ridiculous. I owed one company so much, I would pay them $75 for the month and they charged me $53 interest. Can you imagine how long it would take to pay off a $4,000 balance at that rate? That's what you call a never-ending credit battle.

One time, my brother flew up from North Carolina and told me he only paid $38 for his flight. Of course, he had to explain to me how he uses credit to work for him and earns points on his credit card. I wanted to do that too, but was denied several times, still I did not give up. I finally began to realize that credit was designed as a temporary assistance for a few days or weeks but was to be paid off within the month, or as soon as possible. That is why interest is charged on your balance after approximately 30 days. So, to improve your credit score, PAY OFF your credit card balance BEFORE you are charged interest.

Don't just use credit cards because they came in the mail, but find cards that reward you for using them, like my brother did with the airlines credit card. Also, there are cards that pay you 5% cash back when you use their card for purchases. That's not difficult, especially if you always shop at a particular store, like me with Walmart or Amazon. Again, the secret is to only charge what you know you can pay off before the interest is charged, otherwise you lose all the benefits of boosting your credit score and the extra cash back rewards, because if you are charged 25% interest, did it really matter that they gave you 5% cash back.

To improve your score, start by paying your bills on time and if you do have credit cards, keep your balances low, and try to pay them off as soon as possible. That is basically how I was able to save money for my second house, because I wasn't paying excessive interest on credit cards, I was able to put more money into my savings account. Start slowly, tackling small debts one-by-one, take small steps, don't beat yourself up because of past mistakes, and never give up trying.

> **The godly may trip seven times, but they will get up again. But one disaster is enough to overthrow the wicked. Proverbs 24:16**

What a wonderful Father we have, who can turn our negatives into positives. Please help us to constantly seek your face Lord for guidance and direction along our financial journey and may our light shine so brightly that others will know like Moses that we have been with you Father. In Jesus name we pray.

Managing Debt

Everything so far comes down to having faith and believing that God will help with the information, knowledge and wisdom to *Improve our Financial Story,* especially when it comes to our debt.   Debt reduction takes time but it's not impossible, because we have a powerful ally in Jesus, who is always with us and will never forsake us. How often have you wondered if you can really do this?

I can do all things through Christ who strengthens me. Philippians 4:13

Still even the sound of the word "Debt" isn't appealing, one thing for sure, once you get it, it's hard to get rid of it. But there is one thing the scriptures tell us when we are facing difficulties, trials, or hardship in Romans 8:37:

Yet in all these things we are more than conquerors through Him who loved us.

Webster's Dictionary describes conqueror as, "to get control of as by winning a war, to overcome, or defeat." We just read that we more that conquerors, more than able to win the war on debt, more than able to overcome our past financial failures, and able to defeat poor spending habits, because of Christ in us and working through us.

The Word goes on to say what can "separate us from the love of God which is in Christ Jesus our Lord", surely not debts, loans, or credit accounts. The TRINITY is on our team with supernatural power. As I'm reading all the scriptures, of course another comes to mind, "Faith comes by hearing, and hearing by the word of God" (Romans 10:17). For faith to kick in, you have to hear it, and we are not talking about just hearing sound or noise, but we are talking about hearing the word of God. So, when you begin to feel doubt that you'll never be able to get rid of debt, that you've made many poor credit choices, or your credit will never improve, then find a scripture, better yet, find many scriptures and read them out loud knowing the Word is true. Don't worry about what others are thinking, shout it out until your faith grows, until you believe that you are more than a conqueror through Christ.

The next step is faith, as described in James 2:14-17, and faith is an action word:

What does it profit, my brethren, if someone says he has faith but does not have works? Can faith save him? If a brother or sister is naked and destitute of daily food, and one of you says to them, "Depart in peace, be warmed and filled," but you do not give them the things which are needed for the body, what does it profit? Thus, also faith by itself, if it does not have works, is dead.

Just having faith and not doing anything else won't get the job done. You can't just say "depart debt" and it will disappear; sacrifice has to be part of the equation. How many times did you say you wanted to *Improve your Financial Story*? Maybe you didn't put it that way, but you wanted your finances to be better, if not for yourself, for your children. Did you start working on it right away or did you procrastinate and drag things out until they got worse?

Faith without works is dead. Yes, God will do it all, but we have to be a part of the plan. I heard Pastor Steven Furtick say, "God will not do for you what you can do for yourself." We have to show that we believe by putting our faith into action. Joining a financial eGroup, doing the lesson plans, creating a budget, selecting ways to follow the budget, investments, and growing a legacy, are all part of trusting God as we strive to *Improve our Financial Story*. All the time we are trusting God, we are moving and working and making changes, not just waiting for the heavens to open and now all is right in our finances. That is possible because we know with God all things are possible, but it's a principle that we have to work towards our goals. You know if II Thessalonians 3:10, "if you don't work, you don't eat", that's a work principle. Another way to motivate yourself and get started was from Charlie Nelson, a profoundly wise young man in my eGroup, "if you never sow how can you expect to reap."

How does faith and action motivate you regarding to your finances?

_____

_____

_____

Credit Repair – Can I do it myself? Let's look at what credit repair is first. Actually, I don't have to look far since the internet is full of information, but be careful, some credit repair you can do yourself for free, and the last thing you want to do is add another bill.

According to *Experian.com*, "Credit repair is when a third party, often called a credit repair organization or credit services organization, attempts to get information removed from your credit reports in exchange for payment." Experian went on to note, "because there is nothing a credit repair company can do that you can't do for yourself, it's better to ensure the accuracy of your credit reports on your own." You don't often hear of companies saying it's best to do it yourself, or maybe they believe it's not difficult to make corrections on your credit report when you reach out to them, if you are willing to wait on hold.

Throughout the next topic, there will be information on disputing and improving your credit score. Before immediately deciding to let someone else fix your credit, attempt to do-it-yourself first. It is time consuming and maybe you would spend 20 or 30 minutes to send a letter or make a phone call about a debt, but that time is beneficial if you are making payment arrangements or disputing charges.

If you have other bills that need to be paid off, reach out to the company's billing department and ask if you can make payment arrangements and begin paying a certain amount monthly. If you do make arrangements, make sure the amount fits into your budget. Don't attempt to pay more than you can. And no matter what keep the arrangements you made, otherwise the company might not be willing to continue working with you, possibly throwing your account further into delinquency or even worse, collection, which negatively affects your overall credit report.

How long does derogatory information stays on your credit report:

Derogatory Credit Removal Timeline
Missed payments: 7 ½ years
Account charge-off: 7 years
Repossessions: 7 years
Collections: 7 years
Student loan delinquency or default: 7 years
Bankruptcy: Chapter 13, 7 years   Chapter 7, 10 years
Foreclosure: 7 years

It seems like a long time for something to fall off your credit report, but it does. My credit score was turbulent at best because I made some poor decisions by purchasing items I could not afford, but somethings that affected my credit were not preventable. For instance, I went from a job where I was paid an annual salary, to a job where I was only paid 10 months out of the year. In the long run it was a good decision to change jobs, but initially having to have two months with no pay, was tough, and I turned to credit cards to fill the gap. Unfortunately, I was not able to repay that debt and it sat on my credit report as a bad debt charge-off for 7 years. I know some are surprised that I admit to not being a perfect Christian and paying every debt, but honestly, I'll tell you on year 8 of my charge-off, when the derogatory report was removed, I did shout JUBILEE, and was grateful when my credit scored jumped up. And now that I have been set free, by God's grace, I do not want to be entangled again in the yoke of bondage, and that is my prayer for you.

Were there times in your life when you had to make difficult credit decisions?

_____

_____

_____

Some steps to reduce or eliminate debt? It's important to know the different kinds of credit we are dealing with that makes up your FICO Score: installment loans and revolving credit.

- Installment Loans – With an installment loan, you borrow money once and pay it off over time – auto loans, student loans, personal loans, and mortgages.
- Revolving Credit Account – is similar to a loan but always available, you can keep borrowing as long as you repay your creditor according to the terms, usually credit cards, store cards, and gas cards.

Now that you have your credit report, identify where to focus your attentions.

✓ Make a list of all your debt, use a separate sheet if necessary

Type	Name of Account	Amount Owed

✓ Begin to pay off the smallest one, paying as much as possible as you pay the minimum amount for the larger ones

✓ Once you have paid the smallest one, select the next debt and repeat, until you have paid them all off.

Some financial debt counselors tell you to pay off the larger debts first, especially if you are paying large amounts of interest every month. If that works better for you, go for it, either way you are paying off debt. For me, paying off the smaller ones do not take as long and gives me a feeling of accomplishment.

Once you've paid off all the credit card debt, try not to return down that road and reenter into a yoke of bondage. But sometimes we do fall back into the same traps, don't beat yourself up, learn from your mistakes, and pray this prayer of forgiveness:

If we confess our sins, He is faithful and just to forgive us *our* sins and to cleanse us from all unrighteousness. I John 1:9

Hallelujah!!! That's the **ultimate debt** we want to get rid of, nothing compares to the grace and love of God, that Jesus paid our sin debt and now we are free. Amen.

A final note, don't be afraid to ask for help, begin by crying out to the Lord first if you feel overwhelmed, next reach out to your church, family and friends, maybe they have a financial counselor available to guide you further. Jesus offered some excellent words of advice in Matthew 7:7-8

Ask and it will be given to you; seek and you will find; knock and the door will be opened to you. For everyone who asks receives; the one who seeks find; and to the one who knocks, the door will be opened.

Are there times when you need to reach out for help? Who do you turn too?

_____

_____

Dear Heavenly Father, despite our debt or mishandling of finances, we believe what You said that we are more than conquerors. Thank you, Father for Jesus, our Way Maker, Heavy load sharer, Promise Keeper, and forever our light in the darkness. Help us to ask, seek, and knock, for you are there waiting to open the door. Amen.

Creating a Budget

You have finally arrived at the meat and potatoes of *How to Improve your Financial Story*. At this point you have:

> ⇨ Determined your amount for Tithing
> ⇨ On your way to being a godly steward
> ⇨ Reviewed your Credit Report
> ⇨ Acknowledged your debts (if any)
> ⇨ Ready to Start your Budget

Now it's time to get started. Creating a Budget is where the rubber meets the road, every item, every bill, every luxury, every dime you spend has to be on the table for review. It's amazing to me when someone says, I'm ready to improve my finances, and I tell them to start by listing all their monthly expenses and income, and after several weeks I have not heard from them. The process of creating a budget is initially time consuming but the rewards payoff.

THREE purposes OF A BUDGET:

1) helps you see where your money is going

2) helps you monitor your spending

3) helps you focus on your financial goals.

Have you ever asked at the end of the month, "where has all my money gone?" Creating a budget will help you see where it goes and following your budget will show you the areas that need modification. Or do you say, "I'll work on it next week or next month". Now is the time to take action and take charge of your finances. Reflect on Ecclesiastes 11:4.

> **Farmers who wait for perfect weather never plant. If they watch every cloud, they never harvest.**

Up until now, if you haven't start working on your budget, what are you waiting for? A farmer who waits for that perfect weather never plants. I know a tiny bit about gardening, and I know for a fact that it is hard to get started, even on a perfect day. I need to have the right tools ready, the best soil, my gloves, a sunny day, and most importantly something to plant. That's only the beginning because then I have to till and amend the soil, plant the seeds or transplants, cover with mulch, and water them. Now do I go in the house and wait until harvest time? No, I have to water as needed and the most tedious part, pull up weeds as they popup, not to mention putting up fencing when other little critters get excited about my garden. Your budget is similar to a garden, it's a lot of work, but the joy you have when you see the benefits is priceless. For my gardening, it's a big juicy red tomato, for your budget, it's enjoying your dream vacation or new home.

> **Good planning and hard work lead to prosperity, but hasty shortcuts lead to poverty. Proverbs 21:5**

Do you want to purchase a home, save for a dream vacation, a rainy day, better yet a sunny day? Having a budget helps you set realistic expectations to reach your goals. Good planning from a budget will help you reach your goals, maybe your desire is not a dream vacation, maybe it's simply to keep the lights and gas turned on throughout the year. No matter, there are no shortcuts, because as stated, shortcuts can lead to poverty.

Another way to determine where your money goes is to look at your bank statements and credit card statements. It used to be you had to pull out all your bank statements and try and save your credit card statements and go through each one checking off items. Nowadays since many things are electronic, you can pull up your statements on your computer, and some credit cards allow you to download your expenses to a spreadsheet. This gives you the ability to sort items by category, I usually do this at the end of the year, you'll be surprised how much you spend by category.

Here are two scriptures which are very helpful in following through with a budget:

> **Where there is no vision, the people perish. Proverbs 29:18**

Does that remind you of your situation when you felt lost in financial worries with no vision as to how to turn things around? This verse is not only true for finances but for anything that requires goal setting; weight loss, saving money, big purchases, even character improvement. You have to see it in order to believe it. Can you see yourself with money in the bank, your bills paid, slim and trim, riding on your boat, or even being a friendlier person? Why is it important to see where you're going? Because when you feel like you won't make it, you begin to perish, but when you can envision your goal, day-by-day you begin to believe that you can make it. Proverbs 13:12 says, "Hope deferred makes the heart sick, but a dream fulfilled is a tree of life." Begin to envision your dreams, we know God is able.

> **My people are destroyed for lack of knowledge. Hosea 4:6a**

My goal is to show you how to create and follow a budget as simply as possible following the word of God as a guide and having Faith that the Holy Spirit will guide you. If you can't find the answer you need in *How to Improve your Financial Story,* search on the internet "How to create a budget" and you'll find numerous suggestions. If creating a budget seems a daunting task to you, there are numerous applications for your phone, *Mint,* is one example. Your church might have a pre-designed budget to assist you. Coming up, we'll create a very simple budget using a basic spreadsheet. If you don't have access to a spreadsheet, you can go old-fashioned and use a pencil or pen and notebook paper. No matter your choice, you won't be destroyed for lack of knowledge because you'll have tools for success.

Write out some goals you would like to accomplish from following your budget:

_____

_____

_____

Your Budget:
Income – Expenses – Savings = Happy Day Funds

The first step in creating a budget is knowing your monthly income. Most of us have incomes earned from employment that are the same every month, especially if you are a salaried employee or on a fixed income from social security, retirement pension, governmental assistance, or other sources. Variable income could be when your hours vary weekly, or you are self-employed, and your income is based on your business earnings. The goal in *How to Improve your Financial Story* is to learn to manage the income God has blessed us with.

Are you concerned about your income and if you will have enough for your needs and your family's needs? Do you believe God is able to first of all know what you need as well as supply what is needed? One very important thing to remember stated in Deuteronomy 8:18a

But remember the LORD your God, for it is He who gives you the ability to produce wealth.

God is aware of your concerns and your needs. Paul reminded us in Philippians 4:19, "And my God shall supply all your need according to His riches in glory by Christ Jesus." Then maybe you are asking, why am I in poverty?

> **Jesus is speaking, "The poor you will always have with you, and you can help them any time you want. But you will not always have me." Mark 14:7**

When referring to the poor, this bible verse seems harsh at first glance. I remember in one class we read over this verse and one of the ladies was from a poor country in Africa and had very little, in fact she had just lost her job. I could see how her countenance fell after reading this verse and I asked her what was wrong. She explained that this verse offered little hope for her future. Yes, Jesus did say that the poor would always be with us, however he continued on to say that we can help them any time we want. We have to be careful when reading the Word and not add something in that seems implied but is not. This passage was actually focused on Mary anointing the feet of Jesus with perfume and Judas said, hey we can sell that perfume and use that money for the poor, when actually he was the money keeper and was stealing money from his fellow disciples (John12:6). Jesus said she chose to do a good think since He would not always be with them, but the poor would.

Deuteronomy 15:10, 11a add another layer to how we can help the poor:

> **Give generously to the poor, not grudgingly, for the Lord your God will bless you in everything you do. There will always be some in the land who are poor. That is why I am commanding you to share freely with the poor."**

Do you know someone who is suffering financially, how are able to help?

_____

_____

_____

_____

It doesn't matter whether you earn a little or a lot, God is the one who gives you the ability, all the more to be thankful and generous, because He promises to provide all our needs as well as enough to share with others. Riches and wealth should not be our #1 priority, instead it should be seeking first the Kingdom of God and all His righteousness, then we are assured that everything else will be added.

Is being rich only about money? I did a bible search on the word "Rich", and it was mind opening for me, there are many ways our Father provides for us to be rich.

NKJV – New King James Version
> Genesis 13:2 – Abraham was VERY rich in livestock, in silver, and in gold
> Ephesians 2:4 – Rich in Mercy, as God is
> I Timothy 6:7 – Rich in this present age, but don't trust in them
> I Timothy 6:18 – Rich in good works, ready to give, ready to share
> James 1:10 – Rich in Humiliation
> James 2:5 – Rich in Faith

NLT – New Living Translation
> Deuteronomy 33:23 – Rich in Favor
> Nehemiah 9:17 – Rich in unfailing Love
> Ephesians 1:7 – Rich in Kindness and Grace

NIV – New International Version
> Psalms 145:8 – Rich in Love
> Proverbs 22:2 –Rich and poor have this in common:
> > The Lord is Maker of them all.

Income

This budget is created with a simple spreadsheet, or you can use a sheet of paper. Always begin with a prayer. You don't have too, but it's seemed appropriate since all our blessings come from our Father.

Enter your monthly income

May God bless our Finances					
Monthly	Budget		January	February	March
Income					
Income					
	0.00		0.00	0.00	0.00

Total Budget Income

May God bless our Finances						
Monthly	Budget		January	February	March	Total
Income - Work	1,500.00		1,500.00	1,500.00	1,500.00	4,500.00
Income - Business	850.00		1,200.00	1,000.00	800.00	3,000.00
Total Income	2,350.00		2,700.00	2,500.00	2,300.00	7,500.00

There are many ways you can start your budget for income:

- Change Monthly to Weekly
- Add more or less lines for different types of Income
- Write everything on paper
- Use an application on your phone
- Use a Budget application on your computer
- Or list Income and amounts only

Income Source	Amount
Work	$ 1,500.00
Business	$ 850.00
Total	$ 2,350.00

The budget amount contains you average monthly income. If you have variable income, you can estimate by averaging what you made the previous year or make a best estimate of what you normally receive. As you can see above, January and February's income was higher than the budgeted income. It's best to make a lower conservative estimate monthly if your income is variable, because you don't want to anticipate more than what you receive, then don't receive it, which would put your overall budget in the red. This will be clearer when we add expenses.

What are ways to increase income? _____

_____

_____

Expenses

Expenses work the same way as income, some are fixed, like mortgage or rent, and some are variable like electricity and food costs. There are many ways you can begin to create a list of expenses; look at last year's bank or credit card statements or save your receipts and bills for one month to give you a better estimate of what you actually spent.

Writing out your expenses sometimes reveals more than what we realized. Are there somethings you can do without, or cutback on? Do you need extra guidance spiritually? Read over Paul's prayer to know God's will not only over our family, relationships, and health, but also over our income and expenses. This is an excellent prayer, and if you ever want to pray for someone and have no idea what to ask God on their behalf, this would be an excellent choice.

So, we have not stopped praying for you since we first heard about you. We ask God to give you complete knowledge of his will and to give you spiritual wisdom and understanding. Then the way you live will always honor and please the Lord, and your lives will produce every kind of good fruit. All the while, you will grow as you learn to know God better and better.
Colossians 1:9-10

Here is a list of expense categories and whether they are variable or fixed expenses, with a standard percentage that maybe more or less depending on your situation:

Category	Type	Percentage	
Church	Fixed/Variable	Unlimited	Tithes, Offerings, Donations
Housing	Fixed	25-35%	Mortgage, Rent, Taxes, Repairs
Transportation	Variable	10-15%	Car payments, gas, maintenance
Food	Variable	10-15%	Groceries, Restaurant meals
Utilities	Variable	5-10%	Electric, Gas, Phone, Cable, Internet
Insurance	Fixed	10-25%	Health, Home, Auto, Life, Disability

Medical	Variable	5-10%	Doctor visits, Prescriptions, Supplies
Debt Payments	Variable	5-10%	High Interest Debt, Student Loans
Savings	Variable	5-10%	Savings, Emergencies, Investments
Personal	Variable	5-10%	Gym, Clothes, Shoes, Hair, Gifts
Entertainment	Variable	5-10%	Recreation, Events, Hobbies, Sports
Miscellaneous	Variable	5-10%	Childcare, School, Other Expenses

Overall, the percentages add to 100%, plus or minus, but these categories are only guidelines to get started. Each category has expenditures that make up that category, for example housing would include your mortgage, rent, property taxes, maintenance inside and out, and other home repairs. Your expense budget can have more or less categories and your variable and fixed expenses can be different.

The percentages are only guidelines to what the industry standard is for a particular category. It also gives you an idea if one of your categories is way over the standard. For instance, at one time in 2008, my mortgage made up 50% of my income. At that time, I was paid bi-weekly and had to use my entire check at the beginning of the month to pay the mortgage. I knew I was struggling, but I was not aware that 25-35% was the best range for housing expenses. Remember, you are creating a unique budget specifically designed for you.

Notice that Savings is included as an expense and can include your actual savings and you can further break the category down to include money for an emergency fund, as well has money for investments. Our goal in *How to Improve your Financial Story* is to grow our savings in order to fulfill our goals and dreams. It is always important to set aside money in savings, even at the cost of other categories that might have to be reduced through sacrifice.

Dear Father, thank you for all you provide, guide us as we begin to design our budget, and may all we do and all we have, glorify You. In Jesus name we pray.

A Sample Budget

May God bless our Finances				
Monthly	Budget	January	February	March
Income - Work	1,500.00	1,500.00	1,500.00	1,500.00
Income - Business	850.00	1,200.00	1,000.00	800.00
Total Income	2,350.00	2,700.00	2,500.00	2,300.00
Expenses				
Church	240.00	240.00	240.00	240.00
Groceries	200.00	250.00	175.00	120.00
Restaurants	50.00	100.00	25.00	20.00
Personal Care	25.00	100.00	25.00	20.00
Mortgage	900.00	900.00	900.00	900.00
Electric	75.00	70.00	65.00	50.00
Gas	50.00	100.00	125.00	140.00
Cable and Internet	75.00	75.00	125.00	75.00
Phone	50.00	50.00	50.00	70.00
Travel - Gas	100.00	150.00	140.00	120.00
Auto Payment	400.00	400.00	400.00	400.00
Credit Card - #1	50.00	50.00	50.00	50.00
Credit Card - #2	75.00	75.00	75.00	75.00
Savings	60.00	60.00	60.00	60.00
Total Expenses	2,350.00	2,620.00	2,455.00	2,340.00
Net	0.00	80.00	45.00	-40.00

Let's examine some important aspects of our Budget. Column 1 shows the line items that make up the budget, remember you can change any item to reflect a clear picture of your expenditures. Column 2 is the yearly budget you designed based on your estimated income and your estimated monthly expenses. However, the net was $80 for January (positive), $45 for February (positive), and $40 for March (negative), that's because, for this budget, income and expenses fluctuate monthly.

And in a normal budget there will be fluctuations, that's why creating a budget takes continuous adjustments. I have budgets that go back to 2012 on this computer and on a disk to around 2005. I can see the progression over the years and how God has faithfully blessed and provided for me, as He will for you.

As you can see in the table below, the sample budget had $60 per month for savings, but because of the leftover and shortage, the budget was updated. In this case, instead of saving $180 for three months, a total of $265 was saved.

Month	Savings Budget	Leftover (Shortage)	Added to Savings
January	$60	$80	$140
February	$60	$45	$105
March	$60	-$40	$20
	$180	$85	$265

Now our budget can be adjusted to include the new totals for savings. This brings the net budget to zero, because the leftover amounts for each month were added into savings thereby creating a balanced budget between income and expenses.

Monthly	Budget	January	February	March	Total
Savings	60.00	140.00	105.00	20.00	265.00
Total Expenses	2,350.00	2,700.00	2,500.00	2,300.00	7,500.00
Net	0.00	0.00	0.00	0.00	0.00

When your income is fixed there should be less fluctuations. In this budget, the income increased by $350 in January and $150 in February, but so did some expenses. Which expense lines had increases or decreases:

- Groceries
- Restaurants
- Personal Care
- Electric
- Gas

54

- Cable and Internet
- Phone
- Travel – Gas

It's normal for grocery costs to fluctuate during the holidays or certain times throughout the year, especially if you often entertain guests. Sometimes the economy plays a role in the price of groceries which you have no control over, however you can look for savings with coupons, weekly sale items, or discount days for seniors or military personnel. If you have a favorite grocery store, download the app for even more savings.

Restaurant prices also fluctuate with the economy. If, your budget can allow, it's acceptable to dine out from time to time, but if you're looking to reduce expenses, sometimes cooking at home is more cost effective.

Personal care includes items which maintain personal health and well-being, things like hair care, gym memberships, spa treatments, and more. Depending on your needs, this budget line can fluctuate accordingly. Include some personal items you enjoy; this will help your budget seem less restrictive.

Utilities, electricity, gas, water, and other property user fees can also fluctuate, especially gas in winter months for heating, electricity in summer months for air conditioning, or increased water bill during summer months if you have a garden. If you experience high electric and gas bills, sometimes making home improvements can reduce costs in the long run, i.e., additional insulation, turning down the water heater, or adding insulated drapes on windows.

Cable and Internet costs usually are stable for a few months then increase, always call to find out if there are any specials being offered or if they can apply a discount. Some cable or phone companies pay you to switch, I know of someone who does that after their contract ends or the bill increases. Sometimes mentioning that you are willing to switch will prompt them to offer a discount.

Automobile Gas prices are extremely volatile depending on the economy and world events, even shortages as we learned in the pandemic, but you can always shop around for the best prices. Concerning gas prices, I noticed several stores in the city selling gas at a very high price right across the street from each other, but one mile away on the city outskirts the price was much lower. And it is extremely advantageous if your grocery store offers gas discounts, I've saved from 10 to 30 cents per gallon based on grocery purchases

In our sample budget, several budget lines stayed the same, one example is church, usually this is fixed based on the percentage you decide to give. However, you can always give above that amount, or give an extra offering. Mortgage or rent, is another fixed line, but throughout the year there are other items which could be included that would increase the monthly expense, property taxes, maintenance, home repairs, HOA fees, insurance, etc.

Credit card payments stayed the same, however you could decide to use the net amounts saved in January and February to payoff more of the credit card debt. Eventually when the credit cards are completely paid off, you can place that previously budgeted amount into savings or other investments.

If you notice that your budget is constantly in the "red", which means you have spent more than you earned, examine your budget line-by-line and see where you can make adjustments. Oftentimes it is not easy to "cut" the budget because it requires sacrifices, try to weigh the short-term sacrifices against the long-term rewards.

And don't be too hard on yourself if you miss a target goal or your net fluctuates, God gives you the ability to reassess by honestly looking at your budget. He will provide, but what are you doing with what He gave you, are you being a good steward as we discussed earlier? Or are you hiding or wasting what He gave on items outside the budget, even outside His will, i.e., gambling, or frivolous spending? I am not a judge, and I don't judge those who partake of various activities. My only suggestion is to examine your budget for items which can hinder progress.

This is my opinion only, but if you are faithful over your earnings, a godly steward, following your budget, and have money left over, could you go to bingo or the casino? Ask yourself this, is this a trap or something I can control? If you are in control, you'll be able to follow your budget guidelines. Otherwise, if it's a trap, you'll partake regardless of your budget and often to the detriment of your finances.

What are ways you can reduce your budget lines?

_____

_____

Budget Percentages

Here is our sample budget using percentages to provide further examination of income and expenses, along with economic standards compared to our actual:

	A	B	C
2			
3	Monthly	Budget	
4	Income - Work	1,500.00	64%
5	Income - Business	850.00	36%
6			
7	Total Income	2,350.00	100%
8			
9	Expenses		
10	Church	240.00	10%
11			
12	Groceries	200.00	9%
13	Restaurants	50.00	2%
14	Personal Care	25.00	1%
15			
16	Mortgage / Rent	900.00	38%
17	Electric	75.00	3%
18	Gas	50.00	2%
19	Cable and Internet	75.00	3%
20	Phone	50.00	2%
21			
22	Travel - Gas	100.00	4%
23	Auto Payment	400.00	17%
24			
25	Credit Card - #1	50.00	2%
26	Credit Card - #2	75.00	3%
27			
28	Savings	60.00	3%
29			
30	Total Expenses	2,350.00	100%

Formula to calculate percentage:
Income at C4 =**B4/B7**
Expense at C10 =**B10/B30**

To Copy down use =**B10/B30**
(the $ holds that cell for each formula)

Category	Percentage	Actual
Church	Unlimited	10%
Housing	25-35%	38%
Transportation	10-15%	21%
Food	10-15%	11%
Utilities	5-10%	10%
Insurance	10-25%	0%
Medical	5-10%	0%
Debt Payments	5-10%	5%
Savings	5-10%	3%
Personal	5-10%	1%
Entertainment	5-10%	0%
Miscellaneous	5-10%	1%

Looking over the actual percentages, the sample budget falls into suggested guidelines in all categories accept housing and transportation. Unfortunately, this budget has several categories with 0% used, meaning if the expenses were incurred the budget would be out of balance, either income would have to increase to cover the shortage, or an amount would have to be reduced from another expense line.

This is budgeting in a nutshell; how do you manage what you have to cover the things that you need? It's a slow process that takes lots of trial and error, but a balanced budget is possible.

Use this blank budget to begin writing out your budget:

	A	B	C	D	E	F
1	May God bless my Finances					
2						
3	Monthly	Budget				
4	Income - Work					
5	Income - Business					
6						
7	Total Income					
8						
9	Expenses					
10	Church					
11						
12	Groceries					
13	Restaurants					
14	Personal Care					
15						
16	Mortgage / Rent					
17	Electric					
18	Gas					
19	Cable and Internet					
20	Phone					
21						
22	Travel - Gas					
23	Auto Payment					
24						
25	Credit Card - #1					
26	Credit Card - #2					
27						
28	Savings					
29						
30	Total Expenses					
31						
32	Net					

Thank you, Father, for all the riches you provide. Thank you for the vision and knowledge to create a budget. And even when there appears to not be enough, You promised to supply all our needs according to Your riches in glory by Christ Jesus. Amen.

Following your Budget

What is the Key?

Designing and following your budget will take discipline, but the Good News is that God provides that freely through the Holy Spirit.

> **But the fruit of the Spirit is love, joy, peace, longsuffering, kindness, goodness, faithfulness, gentleness, and self-control.   Galatians 5:22-23**

Creating the budget was the first step, following is where the rubber meets the road:

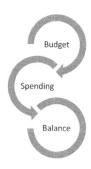

Monthly or daily, reconcile your **budget** with your **spending**, always attempting to maintain **balance** between income and expenses, repeating this procedure until the end of year and next year's budget is created.

Let's review our sample budget at the end of the quarter:

May God bless our Finances						
Monthly	Budget	January	February	March	Total	Average
Income - Work	1,500.00	1,500.00	1,500.00	1,500.00	4,500.00	1,500.00
Income - Business	850.00	1,200.00	1,000.00	800.00	3,000.00	1,000.00
Total Income	2,350.00	2,700.00	2,500.00	2,300.00	7,500.00	2,500.00
Expenses						
Church	240.00	240.00	240.00	240.00	720.00	240.00
Groceries	200.00	250.00	175.00	120.00	545.00	181.67
Restaurants	50.00	100.00	25.00	20.00	145.00	48.33
Personal Care	25.00	100.00	25.00	20.00	145.00	48.33
Mortgage / Rent	900.00	900.00	900.00	900.00	2,700.00	900.00
Electric	75.00	70.00	65.00	50.00	185.00	61.67
Gas	50.00	100.00	125.00	140.00	365.00	121.67
Cable and Internet	75.00	75.00	125.00	75.00	275.00	91.67
Phone	50.00	50.00	50.00	70.00	170.00	56.67
Travel - Gas	100.00	150.00	140.00	120.00	410.00	136.67
Auto Payment	400.00	400.00	400.00	400.00	1,200.00	400.00
Credit Card - #1	50.00	50.00	50.00	50.00	150.00	50.00
Credit Card - #2	75.00	75.00	75.00	75.00	225.00	75.00
Savings	60.00	140.00	105.00	20.00	265.00	88.33
Total Expenses	2,350.00	2,700.00	2,500.00	2,300.00	7,500.00	2,500.00
Net	0.00	0.00	0.00	0.00	0.00	0.00

Normally you review your budget at the end of the year instead of the quarter, but for demonstration purposes and size, imagine this is for the entire year. If you start your budget today, it might not fit perfectly into a total year plan. But no matter what month you start, once you reach the end of the year, there are several totals that need to be calculated. I'm including the formals from my excel worksheet as an example, but if you don't use a spreadsheet, you can use a calculator.

	A	B	C	D	E	F	G	H
1	May God bless our Finances							
2								
3	Monthly	Budget		January	February	March	Total	Average
4	Income - Work	1,500.00		1,500.00	1,500.00	1,500.00	4,500.00	1,500.00
5	Income - Business	850.00		1,200.00	1,000.00	800.00	3,000.00	1,000.00
6								
7	Total Income	2,350.00		2,700.00	2,500.00	2,300.00	7,500.00	2,500.00

To show how to calculate formulas you need to see the structure of the spreadsheet. The top row is alphabetical, A, B, C, D... and so on, these make up your columns. To the left, the column is numerical, 1, 2, 3, 4... and so on, these make up your rows.

B7 has a circle drawn around it, the total is $2,350.00. Let's imagine it was blank and you needed to add the formula, Click the box **B7** then type **=SUM(B4:B5)** this will add the contents starting from row **B4** all the way down to **B5**. This is a short example, but if you were calculating the Total Expenses which has 19 rows the formula would be, **=SUM(B10:B29)** to calculate the total expenses.

To obtain the total for **G4** a horizontal row that adds up to $4,500.00, the formula would be, **=SUM(D4:F4)**

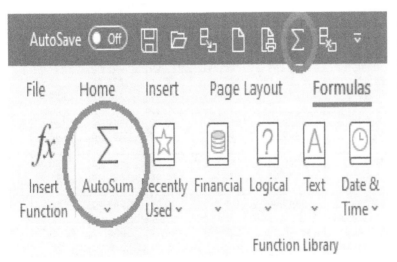

Another way would be to click the box you want to place your formula and click the AutoSum symbol

The program automatically selects a row or column to add based on where your cursor is placed, if this is correct press enter to add the formula

The last area that needs calculating is Average, which is the total of all the months divided by the number of months. Here are two formulas to calculate the Average, this example is using our sample budget, which is only 3 months, if you have more months that is your number, a full budget would be divided by 12 months:

- =+G5/3 this takes the Total in **G5** and divides it by 3 months
- =AVERAGE(D5:F5) calculates the average of **D5,E5,F5**

The good news is once you have calculated the Average column for all the rows, you have your **new budget** for next year. How? Because you took the average of all your months, you now have the best estimate for your yearly budget. Looking at the completed Average column compared to the original Budget column, you see some items increased, some decreased, and some stayed the same. It is your decision if you want to change last year's budget lines. Maybe you know your income is increasing, or you expect to have higher expenses in some categories.

Monthly	Budget	Average			New Budget
Income - Work	1,500.00	1,500.00	0.00	Stay Same	
Income - Business	850.00	1,000.00	150.00	Increase	
Total Income	2,350.00	2,500.00	150.00	Increase	
Expenses					
Church	240.00	240.00	0.00	Stay Same	
Groceries	200.00	181.67	(18.33)	Reduce	
Restaurants	50.00	48.33	(1.67)	Reduce	
Personal Care	25.00	48.33	23.33	Increase	
Mortgage / Rent	900.00	900.00	0.00	Stay Same	
Electric	75.00	61.67	(13.33)	Reduce	
Gas	50.00	121.67	71.67	Increase	
Cable and Internet	75.00	91.67	16.67	Increase	
Phone	50.00	56.67	6.67	Increase	
Travel - Gas	100.00	136.67	36.67	Increase	
Auto Payment	400.00	400.00	0.00	Stay Same	
Credit Card - #1	50.00	50.00	0.00	Stay Same	
Credit Card - #2	75.00	75.00	0.00	Stay Same	
Savings	60.00	88.33	28.33	Increase	
Total Expenses	2,350.00	2,500.00	150.00	Increase	

Whether you increase or decrease your budget lines, the most important thing is Following your Budget. Remember this formula:

Budget:
Income – Expenses – Savings = Happy Day Funds

With happy day funds, you can buy a cup of coffee, splurge on a new purse, see a movie, whatever suits your fancy. Until then, every dime in your budget is important and should be accounted for before being spent. It takes a while to get used to doing this, but in time you'll reap the benefits of being debt-free or have manageable debt, which is rewarding and a praise-worthy accomplishment.

Steps to Following your Budget

1. Income – Most people have direct deposit for safety reasons and timeliness. If you don't have a bank account and use a check cashing place, now is the time to consider having one. Usually if you have direct deposit the bank does not charge a monthly fee for your checking account.

2. Monitor your spending – The fixed expenses normally stay the same each month, the variable expenses require attention. For example, groceries are budgeted for $200, so as you go to the grocery store, be mindful of how much you spend, especially near the end of the month when you've made several trips to the store, because you do not want to overspend your budget line.

3. Enter income and expenses - You can enter line items as they occur, when you pay the bills, or receive income. For me it's easier to complete the budget lines at the end of the month by using my credit card or bank statement, but I'm finding sometimes I can't remember what I purchased if it is a general store. For example, a Walmart purchase, was it for a grocery item or a gardening item? If I entered the expense the same day, I would know. Determine which way of recording expenses works best for you.

4. Set aside time to follow your budget and make adjustments. Time to adjust, time to monitor your spending, time to plan your shopping trips, add up your receipts, then reevaluate often. Over the years I have encountered many people who were ready to get their budget started or should I say, "up and running", but not ready to put in the time required. Following a budget takes more effort than putting some numbers in a spreadsheet or budget app.

I was thinking that following a budget is similar to following a diet or a specific eating plan. You don't want to just eat and eat and eat, because that will produce negative results and be overweight. The same with following your budget, you don't want to spend and spend, because you'll have negative results and be overbudget.

Another example is planting and sowing. Creating your budget is the seed that is planted, following your budget is the seed growing, that does not happen overnight. In the meantime, as we are waiting, remember God is working to grow the seed into the desired outcomes, a healthy garden ready for harvest. We can't get tired while waiting but we have to work by watering, pulling weeds, and removing pests.

Let's not get tired of doing what is good. At just the right time we will reap a harvest of blessing if we don't give up. Galatians 6:9

It's the same with our budget. Once we have a plan, following it is a process, some are able to do this easily and some have to take the longer slow road of modification and reevaluation. Either way it's okay. Progress happens as you move along that road, trying not to compare your progress to that of others. It's almost as if you have to think about everything you purchase and where it fits into your budget plan. But shouldn't you be able to spend your money anyway you like? Yes, you can, but will spending and making purchases outside of a budget constraint help you reach your financial goals, review your financial goals for encouragement and motivation.

You say, "I am allowed to do anything" – but not everything is good for you. You say, "I am allowed to do anything" – but not everything is beneficial. I Corinthians 10:23

Throughout *How to Improve your Finances,* emphasis has been placed on discipline to increase savings for rainy days and sunny days. However, there will be days, times, events, that were not prepared for in the budget, that's where you could use an emergency fund. How much should you save for emergencies and life events that are unforeseen? You have to be the judge of that. Some say you should have two to six months of expenses saved. In our sample budget for two months that would be $4,700 and six months would be $14,100. Those are some very big emergencies. There is never an exact amount, because basically we don't know, only God knows, and as we trust in Him and continue striving towards being a godly steward, Romans 8:28 will prevail:

And we know that all things work together for good to those who love God, to those who are the called according to *His* purpose.

Start small and gradually begin increasing your savings. In this case, the race is not given to the swift, but to those who endure to the end. Proverbs 21:20 makes it clear:

> **The wise have wealth and luxury, but fools spend whatever they get. (NLT)**
>   Or
> **The wise store up choice food and olive oil, but fools gulp theirs down. (NIV)**

Reading through a financial plan called, "It all starts with a budget", one comment was very interesting, "not every dollar is made for spending". Now that is a mouthful. Do you ever feel when you have money or get paid, that you won't be satisfied until you've spent every dime, and if you run out of actual cash, you can always use your credit card? Wisdom is the goal in following a budget, not mindless spending, but thoughtful purchases.

If you are still struggling with following your budget, consider tracking your spending. To get an idea, look over your credit card statements or receipts for a month to see where the problem areas are, or simply grab a sheet of paper. Here is an example of several expenses and the amounts spent for the month:

Budget Amount	Actual Receipts	Total	Over/Under
Groceries: $200	40+30+55+15+60+18	218	$18
Personal Care: $25	15+40+20=75	75	$50
Travel – Gas: $100	40+35+20+15	110	$10

Or put your money in envelopes, and when the envelope is empty, it's gone until next month. If you continually run out of money in a particular envelope, consider adding more money to that envelope or reducing spending. But remember the budget must always balance, so if you add to one line, you have to remove the same amount from another line. Imagine these are envelopes you put your money in:

At one time in my life financially nothing worked: not percentages, averages, coupons, plans, nothing. I had to learn to totally trust in God. It was 2008 and I purchased a home in Lockport during a time when everyone was able to purchase houses no matter what their credit was like. Then people started losing their homes, by the grace of God I did not lose my home, but I did have to struggle.

I was only paid twice a month and in order to pay my mortgage, my whole check and part of my second check had to go to pay the mortgage, so I fell behind on all of my bills and maxed out my credit cards, it was horrible, a financial nightmare. I was really living paycheck to paycheck. At a financial eGroup, someone asked how were you able to make it? I wanted to say something profound and later on that night God gave me this Bible verse that really summed up everything:

For You *are* great and do wondrous things; You alone are God. Psalms 86:10

Doesn't that explain our Heavenly Father. Sometimes words can't explain that God is just Good. I went from paycheck to paycheck in 2008 to having $25,000 in the bank in 2020. Don't ask me how it built up, but that was 12 years, trusting God, slowly saving, not being extravagant in spending, and believing in the goodness of the Lord. God not only supplies our needs but provides our desires as well.

If you delight yourself in the Lord, He will give you the desires of your heart. Psalms 37:4.

I always had a desire to move back down South, something my mother always wanted to do, but for me God made it happen. I thought I could make it happen and one of the ways was writing "The Potato Patch (on Amazon). And when my book did not make the best sellers list, I was confused because that is how I thought my desire would be met, but God had other plans. I had to learn as it says in Zechariah 4:6, '**Not by might nor by power, but by My Spirit,' says the Lord of hosts.**

For God does not show favoritism. Romans 2:11

What He did for me as His child, He'll do for you, because you are His child too. We all see others prospering and maybe wonder, when is my time, where are my blessings. Did you ask? Jesus is standing at the door, let Him in and ask.

Behold, I stand at the door and knock. If anyone hears My voice and opens the door, I will come in and dine with him, and he with Me. Revelation 3:20

I'm not special in my financial story, God is special in His Story, and that's Good News. God is willing to help in all we do, our budgets too.

Final Budget Thoughts

✓ Periodically review your budget. Does it need changes?

✓ Create an emergency fund (usually 3-6 months of expenses)

✓ Follow your plan to reduce debts, when paid off continue setting aside that money into savings, vacations, other monetary goals

✓ Be careful of showers, parties, and other events not in the budget, instead of purchasing a gift, maybe make a gift, do a craft with the family, it makes the gift more personable

✓ Credit cards are not bad, some offer rewards that can pay cash back, but you have to pay off the balance first, then you can reap the benefits of 5% cash back rewards.

✓ Ask for help if needed

✓ Never give up

✓ God is always with you

Dear Heavenly Father, we know we can do all things through Christ who strengthens us, and our budget is small compared to your mighty power and awesomeness. Help us to continue to seek you first Father in all we do, because if it comes from you, we know it is Good. We ask it all *In Jesus' name,* Amen.

Investments

When you think of Investments, what comes to your mind?

_____

_____

_____

Maybe you think of investments as a treasure, something you desire or would like to have. The Bible defines treasures in a distinct way in Matthew 6:19-21

Don't store up treasures here on earth, where moth eat them and rust destroys them, and where thieves break in and steal. Store your treasures in heaven, where moths and rust cannot destroy, and thieves do not break in and steal. For where your treasure is, there your heart will be also.

Sometimes we might focus on investments and money, but Jesus was more focused on the good that we do while here. Where is your heart? A good rule is to look at where you spend your time and money as an indication of where your priorities are. Let's take the stock market for example, if you buy stock in a company, you'll be attentive to any information or news about that company, because you're invested and expect treasure in the form of ROI (Return on Investment). Or, if you say you want to get in shape, but you don't exercise, then do you really want to get in shape, since no time or effort was dedicated to achieving your goal, you won't have a return on investment. The Bible links treasure and heart together in Proverbs 23:26.

My son, give me your heart, and let your eyes observe my ways.

Reflect on ways you give God your heart. Does it line up with your treasure?

_____

_____

_____

I did speak to my brother, a Financial Planner in New York, who stated that Financial Planning and Investing can be different for each individual and depends on what their goals and objectives are. He also mentioned that **IRA – Individual Retirement Accounts**, **College Savings Accounts**, and **Life Insurance,** are all great investments.

The stock market is one investment opportunity that some people enjoy and can be very profitable. When my youngest daughter was born, I wanted to purchase some stocks for her, so I used a company called E*TRADE, which allows you to make stock purchases on the stock market for a small fee, it used to be $9.99. I purchased several stocks based on companies and products I used like, Walmart, Procter and Gamble, Kellogg's, JC Penney, and Southwest. I only purchased three or 4 shares of each stock because that was all I could afford. When the stock market crashed in 2008, and all stocks were down, I purchased five shares of Apple stock, and that was my best investment, because by the time my daughter went to college, I was able to sell my shares and pay for one semester. Here is a quote Elon Musk said on *Twitter,* that was extremely relevant: "Since I've been asked a lot: Buy stock in several companies that make products & services you believe in. Only sell if you think their products & services are trending worse. Don't panic when the market does. This will serve you well in the long-term." I agree wholeheartedly.

Investments are an extremely large category in the world of finance. Of course, we know there are no quick fixes to improving our financial story and all the topics to this point focus on moving slow and steady and trusting God to lead us according to our path. One of my favorite scriptures is Proverbs 3:5,6, **"Trust in the Lord with all your heart, and lean not on your own understanding; in all your ways acknowledge Him, and He will direct your paths."**

Because *How to Improve your Financial Story* is a biblical approach, let's focus on a sure-fire Investments with the greatest ROI and brings JOY (Jesus, Others, You).

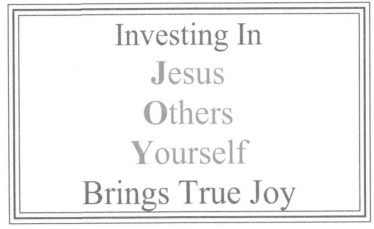

Investing In
Jesus
Others
Yourself
Brings True Joy

In Jesus

Just knowing Jesus is an investment. It's hard to explain the importance of having Christ in your life. Growing up in South Carolina, church was a given, not a choice. When I got older, after my mother passed away, I always remember her telling me, "The Lord takes care of a baby and a fool." It wasn't long before I had a baby, and I definitely knew I was a fool. So, I always looked to God for help and strength, and forty-six years later, I'm doing the same thing. Who wouldn't? The Bible is full of scriptures that God will take care of us, especially when we have burdens, and yes even financial burdens. Jesus explains very clearly in Matthew 11:28-30:

"Come to Me, all you who labor and are heavy laden, and I will give you rest. Take My yoke upon you and learn from Me, for I am gentle and lowly in heart, and you will find rest for your souls. For My yoke is easy and my burden is light."

Are you holding burdens you can give to Jesus?

_____

_____

Webster describes to yoke something is to "join together", who better to join together with than Jesus. And if you know about farming when oxen are yoked together, the load is equally distributed, but Jesus said He'll bear the heavy side of the load. Amen, that works for me. Why carry burdens when Jesus is the Burden Bearer.

Serving God through our offerings, prayer, and service, are definitely ways we are investing in the Kingdom of God, we discussed that thoroughly on the topic of being a godly steward. I'm sure by now you have found a place to serve. If not, what are you waiting for? Investing in Jesus means investing in others, especially since He served us by making the ultimate sacrifice. In turn we are presenting ourselves a living sacrifice, holy and acceptable, which is our reasonable service.

Write some ways you can invest in Jesus.

_____

_____

In Others

The words "One Another", together, appears 524 times in the NKJV of the Bible:

You shall not steal, nor deal falsely, nor lie to **one another** - Lev 19:11

By this all will know that you are My disciples, if you have love for **one another** – John 13:35

Be kindly affectionate to **one another** with brotherly love, in honor giving preference to **one another** – Rom 12:10

Greet **one another** with a holy kiss – 2 Cor 13:12

But if you bite and devour **one another**, beware lest you be consumed by **one another** –Gal 5:15

And be kind to **one another**, tenderhearted, forgiving **one another**, even as God in Christ forgave you – Eph 4:32

Let us think of ways to motivate **one another** in acts of love and good works – Heb 10:24

Be hospitable to **one another** without grumbling – 1 Pet 4:9

Apparently, through the many scriptures in the Word of God it is important that we invest in one another. One thing that occurred during the pandemic of 2020 was the isolation of people. We were not able to gather in church, or if we did, we definitely could not "greet all the brethren with a holy kiss," (I Thessalonians 5:26). We could not hang out together at work, nor could we smile and greet our neighbors at the grocery store. The pandemic created lots of lonely people.

Now as things began to improve and we are able to gather once again, safely of course, we still might not do the "holy kiss", but we can greet our brothers and sisters with a nod if you have on a mask and they can't see your smile. Or you can, "smize" with your eyes. There appears to be a growing culture of detachment, maybe this is acceptable for the world, but not for God's children who are instructed to meet together and invest in one another.

> **And let us consider one another in order to stir up love and good works, not forsaking the assembling of ourselves together, as in the manner of some, but exhorting one another, and so much the more as you see the Day approaching. Hebrews 10:24,25**

A commentary by Chuck Smith on the BlueLetterBible.org, explains this scripture very well, "Regular gathering with other Christians helps to keep the whole body of believers functioning and developing properly." *The Day approaching* is the day of the second coming of Christ, and we want to be ready when He comes.

Another important aspect of "one another" is maintaining loving and caring relationships. Do you have an issue with someone who hurt you in the past? Do you find yourself saying, "I can forgive them, but I can't forget?" Forgiveness is extremely important to building and maintaining relationships with one another. Not only does our model prayer say, **"Forgive us our debts as we forgive our debtors,"** (Matthew 6:12). But God continually clears our slate, through Christ, keeping us in right fellowship with Him, as explained below:

> **He has not dealt with us according to our sins, nor punished us according to our iniquities. For as the heavens are high above the earth, so great is His mercy toward those who fear Him; as far as the east is from the west, so far has He removed our transgressions from us." Psalms 103:10-12**

How much does God forgive us? As far as the east is from the west, God doesn't remember our transgressions, because Jesus paid it all. I'm very thankful for God's grace. Who are we to hold unforgiveness towards a person who hurt us? And if you have to hold a wrong done to you, where would you hold it? If you hold it in your heart, you can develop palpitations or worse heart problems; if you it in your head, you can develop headaches or migraines; if you hold it in your stomach, you can develop ulcers or indigestion. Holding wrongs will eventually harm you more than the person who committed the offense, and they probably don't even remember what happened or not aware that the issue is eating you up on the inside.

When we invest in others, we make room for more, read the story of Elisha and the Widow's Oil in **2 Kings 4:1-7**, where the creditor was coming demanding payment of debt, sound familiar. She was obedient to what the Prophet told her, and God blessed what she had, empty jars, which were used to pay off her debt.

Investing in one another always pays dividends with rewards for the present and future, so much so that it will be overflowing in our lives to others.

> Judge not, and you shall not be judged. Condemn not, and you shall not be condemned. Forgive, and you will be forgiven. Give, and it will be given to you: good measure, pressed down, shaken together, and running over will be put into your bosom. For with the same measure that you use, it will be measured back to you. Luke 6:37-38

Giving, not only money, but love, kindness, and joy are part of a godly principle that keeps coming back to you, the more you give, the more it returns to the point of overflowing.

Finally simple gestures like sending a thoughtful card, a small gift, a word of encouragement, or reaching out to friends or family you haven't heard from or spoken too in a while are all great ways to share loving kindness to others. Hebrews 10:24 puts it this way:

Let us think of ways to motivate one another to acts of love and good works.

Write some ways you can invest in One Another

_____

_____

_____

_____

Did you know that there are five different ways to show love, a concept created by Dr. Gary Chapman, called "love languages"?

Words of Affirmation
Acts of Service
Receiving Gifts
Quality Time
Physical Touch

Some people prefer words of affirmation like, "you're doing a great job". For me it's acts of service, because I'm often in need of help, but don't like to ask. Others prefer receiving gifts, or spending quality time with them, and others, like my son and his family enjoy hugs and kisses. Showing love can be different for each person, so, it's important to get to know someone to really understand their love language.

Dear Father, thank you for opening our eyes to the needs of others. Help us to spread your live Jesus in all we do so that others will see Your goodness and glorify our Father in heaven. Amen.

In Yourself

Are you a person who looks after everyone else, running here, running there, and doing this and doing that, for others? Obviously, there is nothing wrong with helping others, but are you taking care of yourself also? The final step in having Joy in Investments is to invest in yourself. How does that begin? First by loving yourself. We love others but do we love ourselves? That's important also, because you can't love your neighbor if you don't first love God, who is love, then Love Yourself. For some people, including myself, loving ourselves can be hard to do.

Does the Bible say love yourself? Leviticus 19:34, talking about foreigners or strangers in your land, says to **"love them as you love yourself,"** because the Israelites were once foreigners in the land of Egypt, God expected them to know how to treat foreigners when they came to their land. How do we treat foreigners? Are we loving them as we love ourselves?

In addition to loving ourselves, the Bible also mentions the importance of "loving your neighbor as yourself":

Matthew 19:19	**Matthew 22:39**
Mark 12:31	**Luke 10:27**
Romans 13:9	**Galatians 5:14**
James 2:8	

Seems like loving yourself and neighbors is extremely important to our Father in heaven, therefore it's wise to invest in ourselves all the while, loving our neighbors. Here is a scripture that helped me to love myself:

I will praise You, for I am fearfully and wonderfully made. Psalms 139:14

It's important to remember that God made us and knew us even when we were in our mother's womb. Every pimple, crooked toenail, every ache and pain, He knows us, and loves us so much that He made a way to reconcile us to Himself, "For God so loved the world that he gave his one and only Son, that whoever believes in him shall not perish but have eternal life." (John 3:16)

75

That is why we can love others and ourselves, because God first loved us, even while we were yet sinners, Christ died. Take a few moments to think on the goodness of the Lord and read what Jesus said when asked what was the Greatest Commandment?

> The most important commandment is this: 'Hear, O Israel: The Lord our God, the Lord is one. Love the Lord your God with all your heart and with all your soul and with all your mind and with all your strength.' The second is this: 'Love your neighbor as yourself.' There is no commandment greater than these." Mark 12:29-31

Investing in yourself and loving yourself is a topic that can take weeks to discuss. Here is a resource that has numerous plans to help you if you still need guidance, the YouVersion Bible App. Here are a few of the plans that came up when I typed in "love yourself":

Self-Love: 3 Ways to Love Yourself   Alone but not Lonely
Loving your Neighbor as Yourself   The way God Loves You
God made You to be You   Don't Second Guess Yourself
Letting Love In: How God Crushes Your Inner Critic

Usually, each plan takes three to five days to complete, and all are biblically based. We are only touching the tip of the iceberg on how to invest in yourself, maybe it's doing one of these Bible plans, or joining an eGroup, or spending more time in the Bible, or maybe its cuddling up with a good book after a candlelight bubble bath.

Melanee, from one of my group sessions, reminded me that "eating healthy is a great investment". And don't forget the other favorite that goes hand in hand, Exercise.

Think of some ways you can invest in Yourself _____

_____

_____

Dear Heavenly Father, thank you for giving us Jesus our best investment and hope for now and to come. Help us to invest in others and ourselves so the light of Christ will radiate to a world in search of answers that You provide us daily in your Word and in Your fellowship. Amen.

Legacy

What do you think of when you hear the word, Legacy?

_____

_____

Webster's Dictionary defines legacy as: 1) a gift by will especially of money or other personal property, 2) something transmitted by or received from an ancestor or predecessor from the past.

When we are born into this world our family economic status is an indication of our potential status. Of course, there are Cinderella stories from poverty to the palace, unfortunately that is not the norm. The Bible says that we have a wealthy benefactor.

> **And now that you belong to Christ, you are the true children of Abraham. You are his heirs, and God's promise to Abraham belongs to you. Galatians 3:29**

How do we become children of God and joint heirs with Christ?

> **But to all who believed him and accepted him, he gave the right to become children of God. They are reborn – not with a physical birth resulting from human passion or plan, but a birth that comes from God. John 1:12-13**

God gives us the ability to obtain wealth. Here are some ways we can leave and be assets to those we are responsible for, or wish to be a blessing too:

Life Insurance – Baby Boomers and their parents placed more emphasis on having life insurance, especially since like my mother, they grew up during the depression and times were difficult, so they wanted to make sure they were buried properly. Unfortunately, today less people purchase life insurance. No one really wants to talk about death and funerals, but it's good financial planning to at least have the means to bury yourself, either with life insurance or enough money in a bank account to cover expenses.

Will – Making a will can be as expensive as hiring a lawyer, or downloading a form, or writing your desires in a notebook, like my middle daughter. Having a will prevents confusion when you are no longer with us. Simply, title the document as your will and that it reflects your final wishes, name someone to carry them out, who gets what, name a guardian for children and pets, and don't forget to sign the will.

College Savings Plan – Legally known as "qualified tuition plans" sponsored by states and other institutions, normally called 529 plans, because they are authorized by Section 529 of the Internal Revenue Code due to the tax benefits. These savings plans give you an opportunity to set aside money for college expenses for your children. But there are several things to remember, the funds can only be used for educational expenses otherwise you'll incur penalties, and there are penalties for early withdrawal of funds.

Real Estate - Being able to leave land or property to our family is truly a blessing. Times are very difficult presently and oftentimes renting a home or apartment is more expensive than buying a home. The problem is banks and lending agencies require a large down payment to purchase a home which most people do not have, especially when you are first starting out, but with God all things are possible. Do some research before you just say you don't have enough for a deposit. There are programs that offer little or no deposits, like FHA (Federal Housing Administration) loans, First-time Home Buyer programs, USDA (United States Department of Agriculture) loans, and VA (Veteran's Administration) loans.

Savings Account – When I was growing up, and some schools still do, we had school banking where students learned early about the importance of saving money. We also learned how to set aside some of our allowance to give in Sunday School. Even if your school doesn't have a program, check with your bank to see if they have a children's saving program. You can start early with your child about money management and teach them the principles found in *How to Improve your Financial Story* at an early age.

Plant a Tree – I bet you didn't see that coming, but what an awesome idea. Of course, you want to have your own land to plant the tree on. You'll be amazed how excited your children will be to participate in planting and watching the tree grow. If possible, plant a fruit tree for an added return on investment. You can do the same with a **Garden**. If you don't have the land, you can do container gardening on a patio or balcony. One person in my eGroup grows sprouts in her apartment. Children would love to watch the seeds grow in very little time.

Volunteer – Have you ever served at a soup kitchen or gave out toys to needy children? Giving back by donating your time and service is rewarding to those you service and to yourself. Volunteering is a great opportunity to show your children how to share with others less fortunate and create lasting memories. Check with your church for opportunities to serve.

Spend Time – What a way to make lasting memories and show love. Raising my children as a single mom was difficult at times. Growing up my son loved sports, especially baseball and football and I was at every game, from little league through high school. Many days I was the only parent, but I knew he appreciated seeing me, and afterwhile the other kids did as well. Sometimes you're not just supporting your child, but you can fill in the gap and support others also.

Everyone desires to leave something for their children when they are no longer available to support them, but sometimes it's not always money or houses. My mother passed away when I was a teenager and we did not have lots of money, so there was no large inheritance. However, she inspired my life with her love, kindness, and compassion for others, beyond what wealth or possessions could ever provide.

A true legacy is knowing God and passing your knowledge on to your children and impacting the lives of others. John Maxwell who wrote many books on leadership, said this about legacy, "If you are successful, it becomes possible for you to leave an inheritance for others. But, if you desire to create a legacy, then you need to leave something _in_ others." That is what my mother did in my life and that is also my goal for my children and grandchildren.

The word of God explains clearly how to pass on a legacy of faith, hope, love, and generosity to the next generation so they can live holy as children of God.

> **You must love the Lord your God with all your heart, all your soul, and all your strength. And you must commit yourselves wholeheartedly to these commands that I am giving you today. Repeat them again and again to your children. Talk about them when you are at home and when you are on the road, when you are going to bed and when you are getting up.**
> **Deuteronomy 6:5-7**

Jesus quoted part of this scripture in Mark 12 that we mentioned earlier, however this scripture continues by including our children and the importance them knowing about our love for God and the relationship we should have with Him.

With our legacy we can begin to share our stories of the goodness of the Lord with our children who need to know how we overcame adversity, how we persevered through hard times, how we never gave up while trusting in our faithfulness to God.

My culture is rich with stories of how my ancestors made it through the struggles of slavery by God's grace, often singing songs about freedom; *Swing Low Sweet Chariot, Steal Away, Wade in the Water,* or pain and heartache like*, nobody knows the trouble I see.* There were also funny stories like Briar Fox and Briar Rabbit. Dance, family gatherings, travelling South, were all part of my legacy growing up. Also, our Jewish brothers and sisters who made it through the holocaust with great stories of perseverance and through the grace of God were able to overcome.

I will open my mouth with a parable; I will utter hidden things, things from of old— things we have heard and known, things our ancestors have told us. We will not hide them from their descendants; we will tell the next generation the praiseworthy deeds of the LORD, his power, and the wonders he has done. Psalm 78:2-4

Share with your children what God has done in your life. Some cultures keep their history alive by explaining their past. You can't expect someone else to tell your history better than what you can tell yourself. That is what I attempted to do with my book, *The Potato Patch,* which tells the story of Black culture in the 1950's.

I have no greater joy than to hear that my children are walking in the truth. III John 1:4

How will your children walk in truth if you do not share your life story, your accomplishments as well as your defeats. Now that I have the opportunity, I want to begin working on this legacy with my children and grandchildren especially. We must be honest with our children, let them know about our mistakes, even if we did not know the Lord, or our family environment was not conducive to growing in Christ, but now that we know the Lord, we can begin shining the light of Christ.

Train up a child in the way he should go, and when he is old, he will not depart from it. Proverbs 22:6

Does this verse mean that your will have perfect children who never make mistakes? Of course not, but we can stand on the Word which is Truth that our child will not depart from it. It's important to know what they will not depart from, "the way". Jesus referred to himself as "The Way" in John 14:6, "I am the way, the truth, and the life. No one comes to the Father except through Me." Training our children in the way of Christ, is when they won't depart, because they will begin to have their own relationship with the Father. That means bringing them to church, training them in service, giving, and fellowshipping with other believers, that is when they are not likely to depart from the "way" they were trained. Leaving a legacy is different for each person, it could be good, or it could be not so good, that is entirely up to the parent or person leaving the legacy.

Proverbs 13:22 ties legacy with finances and provides an insight to why it is important to incorporate savings into our budget in order not to consume everything on ourselves.

A good person leaves an inheritance for their children's children, but a sinner's wealth is stored up for the righteous.

What will be your legacy?

_____

_____

_____

_____

How do you want to be remembered by your children or grandchildren?

_____

_____

_____

_____

It's not always about money, of course God wants us to prosper and be blessed, but we are blessed to be a blessing. Our main purpose is to Glorify God in all we do and make Him known to others, including family and friends, through our testimony of His goodness towards us. What a great legacy to pass on to our children and to those who don't know Christ.

Thank you, Heavenly Father, for our greatest gift, Jesus, who came to show us the way, the truth, and the life, our true Legacy. Help us to show everyone around us how the light of Christ shines through us as we spread joy wherever we go. All glory and honor to you, our King. Amen.

Going Forward

How to Improve your Financial Story is more than creating and following a budget but also giving, being a godly steward, investing in God's Kingdom, and leaving a legacy for our children and family. The process does not happen overnight but over a lifetime, but you are never alone, God is always with you and promised never to leave or forsake you.

Budget Reminders

1. Put God first

2. Create a realistic budget

3. Pay your Bills ahead of time

4. Make Credit work for you

5. Use Credit wisely

6. Save for large purchases

7. Continually examine your budget

8. Save as much as you can

9. Be patient with yourself

10. Give God the Glory

What are your plans going forward? _____

_____

_____

_____

_____

_____

Whatever our plans, tithing, being a godly steward, managing debt, creating and following a budget, or investing, we know it's not all about money, it's so much more. Here is the story Jesus told of a person who thought wealth was the most important thing. Actually, someone asked Jesus a question about inheritance, and He turned the question around to "beware of covetousness, for one's life does not consist in the abundance of the things we possess", Luke 12:15-21.

Then Jesus told them this parable: "The ground of a certain rich man yielded an abundant harvest. He thought to himself, 'What shall I do? I have no place to store my crops.' "Then he said, This is what I'll do. I will tear down my barns and build bigger ones, and there I will store my surplus grain. And I'll say to myself, "You have plenty of grain laid up for many years. Take life easy; eat, drink and be merry." But God said to him, 'You fool! This very night your life will be demanded from you. Then who will get what you have prepared for yourself?' "This is how it will be with whoever stores up things for themselves but is not rich toward God."

This person knew they had it going on with so much accumulated there was not enough room to store all their possessions. Do you want to be in that situation? It wasn't so much about being rich but wanting more and making room for more with no mention of God our Father, as evident by the number of I's or my's mentioned in the paragraph. Nor did he have any thought about the life to come. It is not often God calls someone a "fool". I'd rather receive the "well done good and faithful servant" label.

Thinking of a closing summary, I happened to find a scripture I noted for the topic Creating a Legacy, my focus was on verse 25, but I believe Psalms 37:23-26 is a prayer for my family as well as yours:

> **The steps of a *good* man are ordered by the Lord, and He delights in his way. Though he fall, he shall not be utterly cast down; for the Lord upholds *him with* His hand. I have been young, and *now* am old; yet I have not seen the righteous forsaken, nor his descendants begging bread.**

You are taking the first steps in *How to Improve your Financial Story,* and this verse tells us that our steps are ordered by the Lord. God explains how in Psalms 32:8, **"I will instruct you and teach you in the way you should go; I will guide you with My loving eye on you."** This reminds me of a story I tell in *The Potato Patch,* when one of the grandmothers in the story was in the choir stand at church and could clearly see that her grandchildren were acting up in the third row. She stared at them until she got their attention and when she did, she squinted her eyes a bit without breaking her gaze, and they knew to straighten up quickly. God said that His loving eye is on us as we go about our day, not matter what we do. Do you feel Him squinting sometimes when you could potentially go the wrong way? Our Father is always directing our paths.

Going forward, my prayer is the *How to Improve your Financial Story: a Biblical Approach,* helps you to find the path to financial freedom, it's really a lifelong process, but you are not doing this by yourself, this book is filled with encouraging scriptures. Now you can begin to add your own verses that guide you and teach your children and others the way, not only financially, but through sharing the Good News of Jesus Christ our Savior and how He guided you through with His loving eye.

Dear Heavenly Father, all praise and honor belong to You. Please help us to apply the principles in your word to glorify you in our giving, our service, our finances, and our love for you, others, and ourselves, so that we may be an awesome testimony to the goodness of God. Every good and perfect gift comes from You, in Jesus matchless and marvelous name we pray. Amen.

Epilogue

Thank you for taking the time to read *How to Improve your Financial Story*. I would love to hear your financial story. You can write me at:

ElonEnam11232@gmail.com
or
Visit my website at:
ElonEnam.org

My website has a very unique name I created when I designed some computer wallpapers many years ago. Elon means God loves me and Enam means God gave it to me, in Swahili an African language. Both names were pertinent to all my creativity, because when writing and designing, I could always feel God leading me and directing my paths. Please write or drop a message and share the glorious blessings God has bestowed upon you. And Thank you for purchasing *How to Improve your Financial Story,* I hope you continue to prosper as your soul prospers.

In closing, may God bless you on your financial journey, I pray you find fulfillment, reward, and abundance in all you do as you glorify God in your life. Here is a beautiful prayer of Paul's that expresses my feelings for you and your family:

When I think of all this, I fall to my knees and pray to the Father, the Creator of everything in heaven and on earth. I pray that from his glorious, unlimited resources he will empower you with inner strength through his Spirit. Then Christ will make his home in your hearts as you trust in him. Your roots will grow down into God's love and keep you strong. And may you have the power to understand, as all God's people should, how wide, how long, how high, and how deep his love is. May you experience the love of Christ, though it is too great to understand fully. Then you will be made complete with all the fullness of life and power that comes from God. Ephesians 3:14-19

The grace of the Lord Jesus Christ, and the love of God, and the communion of the Holy Spirit be with you all. Amen.
II Corinthians 13:14

Made in the USA
Middletown, DE
10 April 2025

74028126R00053